THE ESSENCE OF SECURITY

1817

Harper & Row, Publishers
New York, Evanston, and London

ROBERT S. McNAMARA

✳

THE ESSENCE
OF SECURITY

REFLECTIONS IN OFFICE

THE ESSENCE OF SECURITY. *Copyright © 1968 by Robert S. McNamara. Printed in the United States of America. All rights reserved. For information address Harper & Row, Publishers, Incorporated, 49 East 33rd Street, New York, N. Y. 10016.*

LIBRARY OF CONGRESS CATALOG CARD NUMBER: 68-29573

F-S

CONTENTS

Preface   vii

PART I ‡ THIS WORLD WE LIVE IN

CHAPTER ONE   WHERE WE STAND   3

CHAPTER TWO   WHERE INTERESTS COLLIDE   12

CHAPTER THREE   NATO AND THE FORCES

                     OF CHANGE   32

PART II ‡ THE TOOLS OF POWER

CHAPTER FOUR   MUTUAL DETERRENCE   51

CHAPTER FIVE   THE CHOICE OF WEAPONS   68

CHAPTER SIX   MANAGING FOR DEFENSE   87

PART III ‡ WHERE SECURITY LIES

CHAPTER SEVEN   ON GAPS AND BRIDGES   107

CHAPTER EIGHT   NEW MISSIONS   122

CHAPTER NINE   THE ESSENCE OF SECURITY   141

EPILOGUE   159

Appendix I. The Emerging Nuclear Capability of
          Red China   163

Appendix II. Sources   167

Index   169

PREFACE

My seven-year tenure as Secretary of Defense under two Presidents has ranged over a broad spectrum of responsibilities. That, of course, is the inevitable nature of an office which directly employs over four million people; indirectly affects the employment of several million more in defense-related industries; manages roughly half of the federal budget, some 10 percent of the Gross National Product; and in a thermonuclear era is charged with actions which affect not only the security but the very survival of our twentieth-century society.

Since my appointment in 1961 I have felt that the people of this nation, in whose name and by whose ultimate consent all high government officials serve, have both the need and the right to be thoroughly informed on the Department's decisions. The only narrow and necessary exceptions are those matters restricted by the irreducible requirements of intelligence collection or battlefield security, and these items are closely reviewed by the appropriate committees of the Congress.

Because I believe in the public's participation in the overriding issues of security, I have thought that it might be useful to have published in one volume the principles and philosophy by which I have directed the activities of the Defense Establishment. This is being done as I leave office, but I want to stress that these are neither memoirs nor personal recollections. Rather, they are my actual policy statements, edited and adapted for clarity and logical sequence by Mr. Henry Trewhitt, a distinguished writer on international affairs. They are drawn from documents, including the declassified versions of a number of highly sensitive security matters.* I have adopted this editorial method deliberately, for I do not wish to indulge in the luxury of rejudging issues or events after the fact.

Yet my purpose is not simply to chronicle a series of principles and decisions; my object is to urge the individual American citizen to weigh these matters thoughtfully. The dilemma is that as security considerations become increasingly enmeshed in technological and political complexity, the layman begins to feel that the complications are bewilderingly beyond his competence to evaluate. That is an understandable but dangerous mistake for a citizen to make in any free and open society. The mere complexity of a relevant problem does not relieve one of the responsibility of solving it. The truth is that few problems today are more

* I was fully employed by the U.S. Government during the period these documents were developed; moreover, as I shall describe later, I was assisted in their preparation by large numbers of my colleagues who were also in federal service. Therefore I shall accept no income from the publication of this book. Whatever compensation would normally accrue to me will be channeled to a university to support a series of annual lectures dealing with the broad issues of foreign policy and defense affairs.

relevant to the individual citizen of the United States than those of national security.

How realistically we assess the intentions of potential enemies; what purposes and capabilities we assign to our military forces; how wisely we plan for possible contingencies; how accurately we analyze our range of political, economic and military options; how responsibly we apply our force when force is required; how efficiently we manage our institutions; how boldly we nourish necessary and imaginative innovation in political and social as well as technical fields; in summary, how carefully we think through the rational relationship of means to end in the pursuit of the kind of global environment which will permit all people to live freely and to achieve personal fulfillment —these are the relevant problems of defense that every mature citizen ought to ponder.

To think about them profitably along with the solutions proposed, one must begin by understanding the premises my associates and I have followed. This volume blueprints those premises in detail. From them, we have over the past seven years drawn certain central conclusions. They form the foundation upon which we refashioned and rebuilt the Defense Establishment for which we were assigned responsibility in early 1961. As one would expect, circumstances have intervened with the passage of time which have called for readjustments. But we have been able to make these with relative ease, since an essential element of our original concept was to create an establishment that was flexible and responsive rather than fixed and immobile.

Thus the core conclusions of this book are the same as those on which we have based all our major defense decisions under the leadership of two Presidents and on which we have planned as far forward into the future as we can realistically foresee. These core conclusions are:

That the security of the United States must continue to rest on a firm commitment to the policy of collective security, not retreat—no matter what the provocation or what the allurement—into the futile illusion of isolationism.

That although our strategic nuclear capability is absolutely vital to our security and to that of our allies, its only realistic role is deterrence of all-out nuclear or nonnuclear attacks since it is now impossible for either the United States or the Soviet Union to achieve a meaningful victory over the other in a strategic nuclear exchange.

That the doctrine of massive retaliation is therefore useless as a guarantee of our security, and must continue to give way to both the theory and the practice of flexible response.

That the direction of the Department of Defense demands not only a strong, responsible civilian control, but a Secretary's role that consists of active, imaginative and decisive leadership of the establishment at large, and not the passive practice of simply refereeing the disputes of traditional and partisan factions.

That the dynamics of efficient management in so complex an institution as the Defense Department necessarily require the use of modern managerial tools and increasing

efforts to determine whether the "cost" of each major
program and each new project is justified by the "benefit" or strength it adds to our security.

That the Department's primary role of combat readiness is
fully consistent with innovative programs designed to
utilize at minimal cost its potential for significantly contributing to the solution of the nation's social problems.

And that finally the security of this Republic lies not solely
or even primarily in military force, but equally in developing stable patterns of economic and political growth
both at home and in the developing nations throughout
the world.

It is these seven broad conclusions that this volume
establishes. In my view, they and their logical corollaries
are the chief issues that a Secretary of Defense must face
and implement. That is how I have proceeded, and I take
full and absolute responsibility for whatever decisions,
wise or mistaken, I have made during my assignment to this
office.

For the mistaken decisions, I stand alone. For the wise
ones I owe much to a superb group of colleagues. I want to
acknowledge that debt here; the only difficulty lies in sin-
gling individuals out by name. The list is impressive enough
to deserve a chapter by itself: President Kennedy, who ap-
pointed me to the Cabinet; President Johnson, who renewed
my mandate; the extraordinarily talented members of the
White House staff; my Cabinet colleagues; the members
of the Defense-related committees of the Congress, whose
support, constructive criticism and dissent are all essential

to the vitality of the democratic process; my Deputies, Roswell Gilpatric, Cyrus Vance and Paul Nitze; my Directors of Defense Research and Engineering, Herbert York, Harold Brown and John Foster; my Service Secretaries, Stanley Resor, Paul Ignatius, Eugene Zuckert; my Assistant Secretaries—a distinguished group of men of the caliber of Charles Hitch, Alain Enthoven, John McNaughton, Arthur Sylvester, Paul Warnke, Tom Morris, Phil Goulding, Norman Paul, Al Fitt, Sol Horowitz, Robert Anthony; my assistants for specialized matters, Adam Yarmolinsky, Joseph Califano, Jack Stempler, Dave McGiffert, Dan Henkin, Jack Maddux, Henry Glass, John Steadman; the Joint Chiefs of Staff, and in particular, their Chairmen: Generals Lemnitzer, Taylor and Wheeler; my personal Military Assistants, Lieutenant General George Brown and Colonels Sidney Berry, Robert Pursley and Robert Gard; my tireless and tactful personal secretaries, Miss Margaret Stroud and Miss Polly Yates; and all that long and loyal list of others, both in and out of uniform, who have served this Department and this Republic so selflessly.

No man could possibly have been assisted by a finer group of colleagues than I. Working with associates of such high talent and character has been one of the chief rewards of this office. It is to them, and to the host of others unnamed, that I dedicate this volume.

ROBERT S. McNAMARA

The Pentagon
Washington, D.C.
February 29, 1968

PART I

This World We Live In

CHAPTER ONE

✕

Where We Stand

IN the years since John F. Kennedy asked me to join his
new Administration, the military and economic strength of
the United States and its allies has increased dramatically.
But so have the difficulty and complexity of the problems
we have had to face in framing our military policies. These
years have seen the acceleration of trends which will make
the world of the 1970s very different from the world of
the early 1960s.

Since the early 1960s the divisions within the Communist
world, already apparent then, have deepened and widened.
Indeed, there are now not simply two centers of Com-

munism but several: Havana shows little inclination to follow the lead of Moscow or Peking, and is itself trying to lead the splintered Communist movements of the developing world. In Moscow we still see a desire to undermine the institutions of many nations and the influence of the United States. But we find this desire tempered by a prudence powerfully reinforced by a justly held fear of nuclear war.

The new relationships have opened avenues hitherto closed, and also created new risks. On the one hand we find ourselves engaged in a conflict with North Vietnam and its South Vietnamese supporters to preserve the principle that political change must not be brought about by externally directed violence and military force. On the other, we find ourselves engaged at the same time in many forms of peaceful competition with other Communist states. In the world of the late 1940s and early 1950s, when our adversary seemed monolithic, such a situation would have been unimaginable. Yet today it would be as shortsighted for us to fail to seek peaceful accommodation with the Soviet Union and its East European allies—where possible —as it would be for us to neglect our deterrent against Moscow's improved strategic systems.

Thus the circumstances in which we must formulate our military policies have changed greatly from those of the early 1960s. But our goals remain the same. Fundamentally, what is at issue today, as it was a decade ago and as it will be a decade from now, is the kind of world in which we and others wish to live. This nation made the decision at the end of World War II to base its own security on the principle of collective defense. It was done with the hope of helping to create, in keeping with the principles of the United Nations Charter, a world in which even the smallest state could look forward to an independent existence, free to develop in its own way, unmolested by its neighbors, and free of fear of armed attack or political domination by the more powerful nations.

Some years later, in a world already familiar with the gap between Communist promise and Communist reality, and with Communist aggression as well, we tried to achieve this same high purpose by joining other like-minded nations in a series of mutual defense treaties. By the close of 1955 this system of interlocking alliances had grown to include the Rio Treaty in the Western Hemisphere, NATO in Europe, SEATO and ANZUS in the Far East, and the bilateral mutual defense agreements with Korea, Japan, the Republic of China and the Philippines. Altogether, more than forty sovereign nations bound themselves together in an effort to defend their freedom and prevent the further extension of Communist influence and hegemony through subversion and aggression.

Looking back over the history of the last twenty years, I believe it is fair to say that this system of alliances has substantially achieved its purpose. Though the record is less than perfect, the outward thrust of Soviet and Red Chinese pressure has been generally contained and the independence of even the smallest member of the alliances has been preserved. Beyond the immediate objective of these alliances, our adherence to a policy of collective defense has helped us to pursue our ultimate goal: the creation of a world order in which all states, small and large, aligned and unaligned, can preserve their independence and live in peace.

Collective security has had its price, however. The members of the alliances have had to support large and costly military forces for many years, with small prospect of an early reduction. Moreover, we and some of our allies have had to pay a particularly high price, both in lives and in wealth, for the alliances' achievements, first in Korea during the early 1950s and again in Southeast Asia. Clearly the American people have a right to ask: were these achievements worth their cost, particularly in terms of their ultimate contribution to the peace and security of our own nation?

I believe they were. This is a question which can never be answered conclusively. There is no way by which we can determine with certainty what the world and this country would have been like today had we not based our national security policy on the principle of collective defense during the last twenty years. However, we do know that the course of unarmed isolationism and attempted neutrality which we followed prior to World War II was in the end far more costly in lives and property.

While it is conceivable that we could return to a policy of isolationism, it must be recognized clearly that today it could no longer be the unarmed isolationism of the 1930s. In an age of nuclear weapons and intercontinental missiles, when other nations have the capability to strike our homeland a devastating blow with perhaps only a few minutes of warning, no such easy option is granted us.

Nevertheless, one might argue that we could still renounce all our mutual defense treaties, pull back our military forces to our own soil, and build a "Fortress America" so powerful as to deter virtually any enemy or combination of enemies from deliberately attacking our territory. Then we could deal with the rest of the world on a strictly arm's-length basis.

The crucial point to recognize is that it would be an entirely different world from the one we now live in—and an entirely different United States as well. Without dependable friends or allies we surely would have to maintain a larger military establishment than at present. We also would have to reorient our industry and commerce to achieve a maximum degree of economic self-sufficiency, with a lower standard of living for our people and considerably less economic freedom. Most important, we would be living in a far more uncertain and dangerous world, one in which our influence over the course of events would be greatly diminished. It would be a world in which the pressures for proliferation of nuclear weapons and the means of delivering them would be much stronger than they are today. In time, we could find ourselves literally isolated, a "Fortress America" still relatively prosperous, but surrounded by a sea of struggling, envious and unfriendly nations—a situation hardly likely to strengthen our own state of peace and security. Isolationism is obviously an undesirable alternative to our continued involvement in the responsibilities of world affairs and collective defense.

This does not mean that we must assume the role of

world policeman. But it does mean that we must be willing to continue to support those international arrangements which help to preserve world peace, alleviate conflicts among nations, and create conditions for economic and social progress in the less developed areas of the world.

We must hope that our allies and friends also will recognize that the new international situation is far too complicated and threatening for abandonment of collective defense. The principle that every nation should feel secure in its independence is still valid. It cannot easily be ignored in one part of the world and sustained in another. The contribution of individual nations to this goal can take many forms, and there is admittedly no precise way to determine any nation's fair share of the burden. We, on our part, must recognize that some of our friends and allies simply do not have the economic strength or industrial capacity to equip and maintain the armed forces they legitimately need; in fact, a few cannot even meet their military payrolls from their own resources. It is in the common interest that they receive the necessary financial and material support not only from the United States but also from the other more prosperous members of the alliances. There have been some encouraging moves in that direction, but too great a share of the burden is still being carried by the United States.

The position that other nations should do more in the common cause does not mean that I think we should do less, at least at the present time. The severe cuts in the Administration's economic and military aid request made by the Congress in 1967 were a serious setback to the entire collective defense effort.

We must remember that the non-Communist world is made up of sovereign states which have widely differing histories, capabilities and political and economic orientations. Even where these states subscribe in principle to the policy of collective security, we should not expect that there will always be unanimity as to how and by whom that policy should be implemented in any particular situation. Neither is it realistic for us to expect them all to share our scale of priorities. Each has its own particular set of local problems and national aspirations, and each will insist on judging for itself what is best for its people. We must try to guide them in areas where our joint interests are involved, and try to ensure that what aid we give them is effectively used from both their point of view and ours. We do not and must not attempt to force our views upon them by coercion with trade and aid, for this would hardly achieve the cooperation needed for the collective defense of the free world.

I cannot help but feel, however, that most of the restrictions and fund reductions imposed by the Congress on the national security program in 1967 reflect a much more fundamental problem. That is a growing unwillingness to recognize that if the policy of collective defense is to work, we must be ready to pay our share of the price. If this unwillingness is, in fact, on the increase, then I believe that our nation will be much better off if we confront the real issue directly. That issue is whether or not we should continue to base our national security on the policy of collective defense. There is nothing to be gained, and much to be lost, by paying lip service to the policy and then failing to support the programs necessary to carry it out.

In the 1960s the bipolarity we knew in the earlier post–World War II period has begun to disintegrate. Solid friends and implacable enemies are no longer so easy to label, and labels which did useful service in the past, such as "free world," "Communism" and "Iron Curtain," seem increasingly inadequate as descriptions of contending interests within and between blocs. New bonds of common interest are slowly being built across what were thought to be impenetrable lines of demarcation. Yet this trend toward a more pluralistic world, which is in our interest and consistent with our national philosophy, is still only tentative. Within many nations the factions which see advantage in constructively exploiting this tendency are still weak. Part of our job must be to make it evident to potential enemies that this more pluralistic world would have rewards for them also.

But to make our case we must still face them with the prospect of encountering a well-coordinated alliance of nations willing to do battle to preserve their rights to independence and self-determination. Despite the emerging of new powers and the decline of overly simplified Cold War ideologies, collective security arrangements remain a necessity. The strong must still make commitments to defend the weak.

That the American people have become somewhat dis-
illusioned and weary with the problems of the rest of the
world is understandable. For many years we have borne a
large share of the burden of world peace and security, and
of assistance to the developing nations. But we must never
forget that of all the peoples in the world we have the most
at stake. The existence of an open, outward-looking, hu-
mane society in the United States is affected by the vitality
of similar societies elsewhere. Our burden is large because
our capacity is large—so much larger, in fact, than that of
any other nation as to make comparisons misleading. For
better or for worse—hopefully, for better—we are pre-
eminent, with all the obligations which accrue to leadership. Thus, despite the rapidly increasing complexity of
the world of the late 1960s and the foreseeable 1970s, and
the difficult choices it will pose for us, we must not abandon
in weariness or disillusionment our international role, or
neglect to face up to new and old alternatives.

For my part, I am convinced that we must and will judge
unacceptable all the alternatives to a continued dedication
to collective defense. I also am convinced that embracing
the obligations of international leadership need not force us
to divert badly needed resources from the improvement of
American domestic society. Our resources are sufficient, if
wisely allocated and if we have the will, to meet the needs
of the weak and underprivileged both at home and abroad.
For the sake of our security and our well-being, we can
afford no less.

CHAPTER TWO

✳

Where Interests Collide

OVER the years since World War II the United States has developed a range of world-wide interests unique in history. One reason is that the United States has learned much about the realities of nuclear weapons, including their limitations as an instrument of policy. Some of those realities may at last have impressed Soviet leaders, particularly since the confrontations over Berlin and Cuba in 1961 and 1962. In any case, they have not repeated such direct and perilous challenges to fundamental United States interests.

Nevertheless, American and Soviet interests still collide at many points in the world. And there is no comforting assurance as to the direction in which Red China's tremen-

dous potential will be applied as she begins to recover from
internal chaos. Both Communist governments, moreover,
have continued at this writing to supply massive aid to
Hanoi in its operations against South Vietnam.

Obviously our interest in world-wide political and military developments is nowhere keener than on the subject
of goals and policies in the two great centers of Communism. Realism bids us both to seek understanding with
them and to recognize that, in some areas at least, they
remain fundamentally hostile to us despite their own differences. These differences, however, already have had a profound effect on their bilateral relationship, on other Communist nations and, therefore, on the place of Communism
in world affairs.

The fissures have shown no sign of healing. It may be
that no influence short of a change of regime either in
China or in the U.S.S.R. can restore even a façade of unity
across the Communist world. Peking's challenge to Moscow
has generated greater Chinese militancy, and at times
greater militancy in Soviet policies as well.

The strident behavior of the Red Chinese has caused
Soviet leaders to confront the fact that they, too, have an
interest in stability that must be balanced off against continued adherence to revolutionary ideology. Both strands
are present in Soviet policy. The task of creative statesmanship for the West will be to move Moscow further in constructive directions while at the same time working to break
down the wall which insulates Peking from outside influence.

Our own interests have not fared badly as a result of divisions in the Communist world. Both the Soviet Union and mainland China have suffered serious setbacks in Latin America, Indonesia and in the developing world in general. Each is devoting a large share of its energies to its dispute with the other. Partly as a result of Moscow's greater concentration on domestic affairs and partly because of Peking's defiance, the governments of Eastern Europe have been able to assert increasing independence. We may hope they will begin to establish better relations with the West. Over the long run these bonds may ease the defense problem for the entire NATO area. For the near future, however, though Europe is comparatively free from overt threats or pressures, a strong NATO will still be required to keep it that way.

Aside from the purely nationalistic side of the Sino-Soviet dispute, a large number of ideological issues have emerged. Some are unimportant to the United States. The dispute as to how the "world revolution" is to be achieved is of compelling importance to us, however. Since 1962 the Soviets generally have taken a less militant approach than Red China, although they continue to affirm their support for what they call wars of national liberation. The Soviet leadership demonstrated some restraint in its support for North Vietnam and in support of insurgencies in some other areas of the world. In Latin America, for example, it apparently opposes Fidel Castro's policy of externally supported armed insurrection, choosing instead to compete for influence over the indigenous Communist parties and seeking to expand Soviet presence and relations with Latin-

American governments. By contrast, Red Chinese leaders enthusiastically endorse Castro's efforts to apply their doctrine of "peoples' wars."

There remain, nevertheless, many problems between the United States and the Soviets, some old and some new. Independently of their disagreement with the Chinese, or perhaps partly because of it, the Soviet leaders continued to support Hanoi in Southeast Asia. That may have been one reason they were less willing to cooperate with the United States in other areas of policy, such as the mutual reduction of forces in Europe or arms-control measures. It seems likely that relations with the U.S.S.R. could be improved once Hanoi's aggression in Southeast Asia is terminated. But until these elements are stabilized, we must do our best simultaneously to preserve the constructive aspects of our relationship with Moscow and guard against counting on improvements before they occur.

To mention restraint in Soviet policy toward Southeast Asia is not to suggest that Moscow's support of North Vietnam is unimportant in historical context. Its support has done much to sustain Hanoi's effort in South Vietnam. Similarly, the Soviet Government must carry a major share of the responsibility for setting off the short but explosive war in the Middle East in the summer of 1967, and subsequently for making the achievement of a Middle Eastern settlement more difficult.

At the same time, Moscow's record over the last half-dozen years includes its initiative to bring about peace between India and Pakistan in 1965, and its generally constructive behavior during the Laotian crisis and the Sino-Indian border dispute. The Soviet leaders also have been willing to incur the sustained invective of the Chinese in their negotiations with us for an agreement to halt the proliferation of nuclear weapons. These are only a few examples, but they serve to point up the mixture of conflict and cooperation in the U.S.S.R.'s relations with the non-Communist world.

The Soviets recently have projected an image of increased activity, determination and new strategic direction, especially toward developing a capability for flexible military response. There are some signs that they are developing the forces required to give them limited mobile military capability to meet some types of contingencies beyond the land areas of the Communist countries. A fully flexible response remains outside their immediately foreseeable capabilities, however.

Soviet developments in strategic weapons such as antiballistic missiles give evidence of a continuing search for security through more advanced arms. But the military applications of Soviet power, such as recently increased naval activity in the Mediterranean, appear to be primarily diplomatic gestures. In that specific case it may be aimed at redressing political losses sustained from Moscow's inability to prevent the Israeli victory over the Arabs. Soviet naval craft in the Mediterranean, including missile cruisers and submarines, have effectively shown the flag, but they have done so without the base structure and support facilities that would be necessary for sustained military operations.

These political and military developments were accompanied by a substantial increase in Russia's defense expenditures, as projected in the budget announced for 1968. The increase of at least 2.2 billion rubles, after allowance for higher prices, bookkeeping changes and perhaps a military pay increase, reflected the continued expansion of the Soviet defense effort. Analysis of budget data for 1968 indicated that this diversion of additional funds to military purposes might force a slowdown in investment in agriculture, industry and possibly housing. Apparently Soviet leaders are willing to risk a lower growth rate in industrial plant and gamble on good growing weather in order to meet their defense needs.

It was not entirely clear how the additional resources for defense were to be distributed among the various military programs. Of one thing we could be sure: the cost of the Vietnam conflict to the Soviet Union would be considerably higher in 1968 than in 1967 unless the level of combat could be scaled down or ended. It is uncertain, however, what effects the increased budgetary levels will have on Soviet military and foreign policy for the near future. The Soviet leaders clearly seek a military posture which will give them capabilities more closely in balance with our own, and the growth of our own power over the last several years has no doubt been a factor in their decisions. For the next few years, however, their abilities to support substantial forces relatively distant from their own frontiers will continue to be quite limited.

Recent events in China reflect none of the careful calculation of the Soviet Union, of course. Since mid-1966 the continuing turmoil of the Great Cultural Revolution has demonstrated how wrong we were earlier in our belief that the leadership was strong and united. Even after the government in Peking sought to calm the hordes of young Red Guards it had unleashed, civil disturbances and armed clashes continued, many of them involving the Army. Industrial production and transportation were disrupted. The educational process was almost completely halted, and government administration at all levels was severely weakened.

It now seems clear that what occurred was an attempted revolution within a revolution. Concerned about flagging revolutionary spirit in the government and party, and concerned that future generations would lose sight of his purist Communist goals, Mao Tse-tung set out to conduct a massive housecleaning. When existing mechanisms proved inadequate, he fashioned a new instrument, the Red Guards, and set them loose against the Communist bureaucracy, the very people responsible for the administration of the nation's day-to-day affairs. The failure of the Great Leap Forward, clearly evident by 1960-61, apparently convinced the bureaucracy that a more pragmatic approach to China's economic problems was urgently needed. This approach necessarily relaxed some of the dogma favored by Mao and caused a return to quasi-capitalistic techniques such as reestablishment of private agricultural plots in the rural areas and material incentives for the industrial workers in the cities.

Whatever the short-term results, China may be years

from full recovery. Mao damaged the Communist bureaucracy, but neither destroyed it nor transformed it into an effective instrument of policy. Administrative control over the nation was seriously weakened, but the Red Guards proved unable to displace the bureaucracy. The Army was called upon to restore order in the cities and to maintain production schedules in the factories, in the mines and even on the farms. Nevertheless, clashes between the contending factions continue at this writing; the economy and the educational system are still in disarray; once again, Mao has demonstrated that it is easier to create chaos than to re-establish order. There still has been no clear evidence of the reunited leadership which is the first essential for repair of the damage wrought by the upheaval.

The damage was by no means limited to the domestic scene, for the Cultural Revolution also dealt Red China's foreign policy a severe blow. Its prestige among the Communist parties has declined precipitously, in most instances to the advantage of the Soviet Union. Its relations with the rest of the world are at low ebb. Indeed, Red China has managed to antagonize most nations with which it still maintains diplomatic relations. Most of its ambassadors have been recalled to Peking as part of the Great Cultural Revolution, while the Chinese diplomatic missions abroad have marked time ineffectively. Sooner or later the present leadership will pass from the scene, but it is by no means certain what such a development will mean to the present alignment of the world. A more moderate regime in China could result in easier relations with the outside world, including the United States, or it could mean a rapprochement with the Soviet Union, or possibly both. Even the second alternative might prove to be of advantage to the outside world if an increasingly moderate viewpoint prevails within the Soviet leadership, in that the Soviets could serve as a moderating influence on Red China. If a more militant approach is adopted by the Soviet Union, however, a rapprochement with China could confront the United States and its allies with a new and even more severe threat.

In any event, mainland China, with a population approaching 800 million, a military establishment of some three million and a growing stockpile of nuclear weapons, will be a power to be reckoned with in the 1970s. In its relations with the Peking government, the United States must emphasize the common interest we share in avoiding war and hope that a dialogue can be started. Meanwhile, we must continue to try to deter direct or indirect pressures against China's neighbors.

Both China and the Soviet Union have deep and conflicting interests in Southeast Asia, an area which also tests the viability of the collective defense policy of the United States. Here, close to Red China, lie a number of small, non-Communist states, each trying in its own way to maintain freedom and independence. The confusion and discord between the Communist capitals is well illustrated in this region. The U.S.S.R. is nominally joined with Peking in supporting Hanoi. Each, however, is seeking to prevent the other from gaining dominance in Hanoi, while North

Vietnam probably wishes to fall under the dominance of neither.

Thus it is possible that Moscow, Peking and Hanoi all disagree as to what the future shape of Southeast Asia should be. These disagreements may have allowed Hanoi, while pursuing its drive to conquer the South, to play off the Soviet Union against China for material assistance. Thus, while a trend toward polycentrism among the Communist nations is generally welcome, there will be cases, as in Vietnam, where it may intensify our problems rather than ease them.

At this time the Soviet leaders may believe that North Vietnam will be an outpost for their more pragmatic form of Marxism and serve as a buffer hemming in the zealots of Peking. If this is their calculation, they are playing a dangerous game: an ultimate Communist victory in South Vietnam would erode the position of many of the non-Communist states in Southeast Asia, and the chief beneficiary would be China, not the Soviet Union. Such a victory would be seen as a triumph for Chinese militancy and as vindicating that position in the ideological dispute with the Soviet Union. In contrast to North Korea, which borders both, Southeast Asia is separated from the Soviet Union by the great land mass of China. It is unlikely, therefore, that the Soviets could long maintain a special position in that area in defiance of China.

But our real concern is not over which of the two rivals will emerge dominant. Our concern is that no great power dominate the area. The United States has no desire to compete with either the Soviet Union or Red China for hegemony in Southeast Asia, or indeed to achieve any special position there. This is not to say that we are indifferent to what transpires on the other side of the Pacific Ocean. Whether we like it or not, we are a Pacific power: our West Coast borders on the Pacific and our fiftieth state lies halfway across it. Moreover, we have important historical ties and commitments to many of the nations in the Western Pacific. We have therefore a vital strategic interest in that area, an interest we cannot ignore.

The turmoil in Vietnam, however, has tended to obscure the substantial progress being achieved elsewhere in the area. Time purchased at heavy cost is being put to good use by the non-Communist Asian states. There is a growing appreciation of the need for collective action to meet common problems, and although the conflicts slowed the Mekong Development Project, it and other regional efforts such as the Asian Development Bank and the Asia and Pacific Council are moving forward. There is a growing network of cooperation among the area's non-Communist nations, both functional efforts focused on common problems and broader ties with more ambitious goals. We can hope these efforts eventually will provide the region with the collective political, economic and military strength that will enable it to determine its own destiny.

Our role in this process will be particularly important. American policy toward Southeast Asia and the Southwest Pacific area must blend concern and restraint as we help the East Asian nations to build among themselves the true security that flows from economic and social progress.

Meanwhile, outright and overt aggression by large conventional forces is unlikely in the region. Internal conflicts, fostered by socioeconomic stagnation, communal disputes or externally supported, Communist-nurtured subversion, are the more plausible threats.

The special situations in Thailand and Laos are particularly illustrative, in view of their relationship to Vietnam. Both of these nations are threatened by externally supported insurgencies. They also are threatened by the debilitating economic, social and political conditions common to much of the area. Yet the Thai Government has assumed a leading role in regional cooperation. It was instrumental in the creation of the Association of Southeast Asian Nations and was a prime mover in fostering closer political consultation and action among neighboring nations. The Thais' own counterinsurgency effort against the guerrillas in the northeastern provinces has improved measurably. This effort, consisting of combined military-civilian police operations, is designed both to quell the externally supported insurgency and to begin to eradicate the factors which facilitate its growth: poverty, illiteracy and long years of minimal contact with the people by the central government.

Internal conflict is greater in Laos than in Thailand primarily because external involvement there is greater. The North Vietnamese Army has continued at this writing to infiltrate south through Laos, and North Vietnamese troops reinforce the Pathet Lao against the Royal Lao Government. North Vietnam has also provided substantial military assistance to the insurgents. But for a number of reasons, including continued international support for the 1962 Geneva Accords and our economic and military assistance to the government of Laos, Prime Minister Souvanna Phouma has been able to maintain a partially successful defense against North Vietnamese aggression.

I believe that over the long run a truly independent, neutral Southeast Asia would best serve the interests of all the nations involved. It would remove one source of strife between the outside world and the Communist nations, and among the latter as well. Moreover, it would create the kind of environment required for the rapid development of the region's basically rich natural resources.

Farther north in the East Asian crescent, the North Koreans have not hesitated to remind South Korea that she lives in the constant shadow of renewed aggression. During the summer of 1967 and in early 1968 there was a substantial increase in the North's harassment and intrusion along the Korean Demilitarized Zone, with the dual objectives of discouraging the South's assistance to Vietnam and of undermining its political and economic stability. Thus far, efforts by the North to organize a guerrilla base in the interior have been frustrated. Nevertheless, we must anticipate that North Korea's aggressive activities, both along the Demilitarized Zone and farther south, will persist and perhaps intensify in the months ahead. The North Koreans are fully aware that as the Republic of

Korea grows stronger, their chances of achieving control over the entire peninsula diminish.

The Republic of China continues to be confronted by Peking's long-held objective of seizing Taiwan. Mainland China's developing nuclear capability, combined with its military modernization programs, has caused increasing concern on Taiwan. Our bilateral mutual defense treaty for the defense of Taiwan remains essential therefore to the security of the Republic of China.

In South Asia tensions have slowly abated, though the two giants of Communism have pursued active policies in the area. While issues remain in dispute between India and Pakistan, we hope they will continue to seek peaceful settlement. In April, 1967, the United States announced a new military supply policy for the subcontinent, under which its previously suspended grant aid was formally terminated and advisory and supply missions were formally withdrawn. No lethal weapons are being sold by the United States to either India or Pakistan, and we have urged both governments to avoid an arms race, to scale down the size of their armed forces and to allocate the savings to essential economic and social programs.

Pakistan's early search for arms resulted in relatively small deliveries from the Middle East and Indonesia and extensive purchases from commercial sources in Western Europe. More important, Red China provided large quantities of small arms, vehicles, tanks, artillery and fighter aircraft, though later she scaled the supply down to spare parts only. In this respect, China's objectives in the subcontinent appear to remain the same: to establish herself as a major political influence in the area, exploiting Pakistan's and India's differences to her own advantage, preventing or delaying the development of a strong India, and minimizing United States and Soviet influence.

The Soviet Union, on the other hand, has tended to concentrate its efforts on India, and only recently has begun to cultivate its influence in Pakistan. In addition to pledging a net commitment of $300 million to India's Fourth Plan, the Soviet Union has undertaken to meet a portion of her defense requirements as well. On the whole, however, Moscow gives the impression it is aware of the dangers inherent in renewed warfare between India and Pakistan and is exercising restraint in military assistance.

Among all the persistent and recurrent issues that burden international affairs, none is thornier than relations in the Middle East. When war briefly erupted in June, 1967, for the third time in twenty years, it left behind many old problems and created some new ones. The United States supported the efforts of the United Nations and used every other available channel to encourage fruitful negotiations. We are continuing our efforts to limit arms deliveries to the area. At the outbreak of the most recent hostilities, the United States suspended all arms shipments; unfortunately, the Soviet Union did not act in similar fashion, and the rapid resupply of Communist arms to the U.A.R., Syria, Iraq and Algeria after the war served only to increase tensions and fears. The Soviet Union's position on Middle Eastern questions, its increased naval presence in the

Mediterranean, its intervention in the conflict in Yemen and efforts to reduce or supplant Western influence generally have further contributed to the instability in the region.

The recent increase in Soviet resources, diplomacy and propaganda directed to the Middle East underscores the importance Moscow attaches to this strategically significant area at the crossroads of Asia, Africa and Europe. In recent years the Soviet Union has sent a considerable portion of its total economic and military aid to the region. The Middle East accounts for a large percentage of all foreign technicians being trained in the Soviet Union. Clearly the area stands high on the Soviet scale of politico-military priorities. However, the Soviets probably do not plan to acquire formally permanent bases in the Mediterranean and the Arab world. Indeed, we believe that those countries which have potentially useful facilities, primarily the U.A.R., Syria, Yemen and Algeria, would resist granting full base rights on political grounds.

To the north, Greece, Turkey and Iran continue to fulfill important forward defense roles, standing between the Soviet Union and the warm-water ports and oil resources of the Middle East. Substantial military assistance to them over the past two decades by the United States has undoubtedly been a factor in discouraging Soviet military adventures in the area. Our grant military assistance to Iran is now being replaced by military sales, but Greece and Turkey probably will continue to need grant military aid for some time. During 1967 U.S. aid to Greece was partially curtailed following assumption of power by the military junta which overthrew the elected government in April.

The Soviet thrust into the Mediterranean and Middle East region also embraces the northern part of Africa. Increasing Soviet activity in North and Northeast Africa represents a potentially serious threat to the equilibrium of both that area and Western Europe. The Maghreb and the Horn are the areas of Africa of most immediate strategic concern to the United States—North Africa covering the southern flank of NATO and the Horn standing at the approaches to the Red Sea and Indian Ocean. Soviet policies in these areas seem designed to reduce or eliminate Western influence generally, to disrupt NATO and Western security interests, and to increase Soviet political, military and economic influence.

The Arab-Israeli crisis and the continued Soviet-supported Algerian military build-up have added to the basic instability of the area. The delivery of over $200 million worth of Soviet equipment to Algeria since 1965 continues to alarm her moderate neighbors. While the present Algerian regime maintains friendly diplomatic relations with its North African neighbors, there is apprehension in the area about her military potential. Our own limited military assistance helps Algeria's neighbors, Morocco, Tunisia and Libya, to maintain a minimum defensive capability.

Closer to home, we have thoroughly reoriented our military policy toward Latin America over the past seven years. Our purpose was to bring that policy into line with the nature and scope of the real threat to the south of us.

We now recognize formally the low probability of conventional attack on any American state from outside the hemisphere. As a result we see no requirement for Latin-American countries to support large conventional military forces, particularly those requiring expensive and sophisticated equipment. Outlays for such forces are an unwarranted diversion of resources from the more urgent and important tasks of economic and social development. Our military assistance policy, therefore, is designed to limit their purchases to replacement items of a kind and at a cost that will improve internal security and at the same time not hinder economic development.

The absence of a major external threat to this hemisphere also has helped us to focus the energies of the Rio Treaty nations toward the widely shared problem of armed insurgency. Indeed, another major change in our policy reflects the need to deal with the threat of externally inspired insurgencies. This threat has been a major challenge to some of our Latin-American allies, and we have tried to help them by providing training, advisers and assistance in the equipment and techniques of counterinsurgency. Notwithstanding the encouragement and sponsorship of such insurgency by Cuba, our allies until now have been able to deal with it effectively wherever it has surfaced. The death of Ernesto Che Guevara in Bolivia in the fall of 1967 dealt a severe blow to the hopes of the Castroite revolutionaries.

But counterinsurgency alone is an inadequate response to this problem. Removal of the causes of human suffering and deprivation is essential if stable political institutions are to flourish free of the threat of violent revolution. This recognition has been the inspiration of the Alliance for Progress, in which we seek with the Latin-American nations to achieve a peaceful economic and social revolution within a generation.

Not surprisingly, most Latin Americans aspire to peaceful revolutions in their societies and their personal well-being. Since they seek improvement without violence, and soon, they need the relatively modest military and economic help we are providing. Without it, prospects for realizing their aspirations would be slim indeed. Still, we should not forget that it is the Latin Americans themselves who are making the principal contribution toward fulfillment of the Alliance for Progress, a contribution involving both hard work and willingness to accept difficult social and political responsibilities. The Alliance is, in fact, a partnership, and it is to be hoped that our mutual efforts in this hemisphere ultimately will yield the freedom and prosperity which we seek for all the countries of the Alliance.

Essentially this brief review has focused on the capabilities, goals and motives of those who challenge us, and on the points of confrontation, major and minor. Happily, in that context I have not mentioned many of the leading nations of the world, including Japan. For Japan, well on the way to becoming the third leading industrial power, has steadily strengthened her political institutions. She has become increasingly active in international affairs, especially in Asia. Though her Constitution is still interpreted as precluding the dispatch of armed forces abroad, security questions are being discussed today with greater realism and candor. Her new national defense plan provides for modernization of Japanese defense forces. Except for passing reference here, I have set Europe aside for consideration later.

I deliberately closed this review with a brief look at Latin America. For it seems to me that the continent to the south typifies the challenge of our times. Its vast resources and its vital population provide the raw material for electrifying progress; its great poverty and social injustice contain the seeds of violent revolution. Here, free of the threat of external aggression, the line is clearly drawn.

CHAPTER THREE

✦

NATO and the Forces of Change

O F all the links in our chain of collective security, the North Atlantic Alliance is the most visible and the most dramatic. As it approaches its twentieth anniversary in 1969, the NATO Treaty has maintained relative peace in Western Europe through a period of severe strain and, at times, acute danger. Its success can be measured far beyond stand-off deterrence alone, for in recent years the immediate external threat to Europe has declined. But in its place have developed perhaps inevitable internal pressures, the lure of a less onerous burden, the temptation to give short-term political and economic issues priority over long-term security.

NATO was created on April 4, 1949, in the wake of repeated and reckless Soviet adventures, including the blockade of Berlin. The government in Moscow had proved unwilling to let its ideology compete freely in the political marketplace after World War II. In effect, the Soviet master plan sought to exploit economic dislocation and the war weariness of Europe and the United States. It called for aggressive subversion and military pressure, which always contain the threat of direct conflict. NATO established the deterrent balance, committing the United States totally to the defense of Europe—and vice versa. Along the way, the original alliance of twelve members was joined from the southern flank of Europe by Greece and Turkey and also by the Federal Republic of Germany.

It is understandable that fundamental questions have been raised about the Alliance in recent years. After all, it seems a long time since that summer of 1961 when Chairman Khrushchev threatened to end with a stroke of his pen the Western presence in Berlin. It was a period of high tension as the Red Army, with a supposed strength of 160 divisions, seemed to tower over Europe. The United States and its allies held firm during that summer, and the winter and spring that followed, and slowly tensions subsided.

Since then access to West Berlin has remained relatively undisturbed. Tensions between East and West have been relaxed; Europe has been a relatively stable and peaceful continent. Sino-Soviet differences widened the opportunity for the East European states to assert their independence of Moscow, and their political and trade relations with the West have become freer. On the whole, then, NATO's first two decades included great change in the area. Generally, in both military and political terms, these developments favored the Western nations, encouraging a growing sense of security.

Indeed, some authorities in both the United States and Western Europe seem to believe that the military threat to Western Europe has largely disappeared. Some may even suppose that the Soviet Union has mellowed to the point that NATO's utility as a military alliance has all but vanished. As a result, despite an enormous increase in European wealth, defense budgets generally receive a decreasing share of that wealth.

Clearly, the thawing process between East and West is well advanced on both sides of the Elbe. But this process does more than open up new opportunities to reduce tensions in Europe. It also confronts us with new problems, particularly as to how best to maintain our unity during the period when old positions, attitudes and relationships are being re-examined. If the Alliance is in trouble, it may well arise from an exaggerated sense of security.

We have made abundantly clear our desire to build bridges between East and West, to heal the division of the continent, including Germany. The United States will grasp every real prospect for better relations with the countries of Eastern Europe and the Soviet Union. We are committed to the reconciliation of Europe and have no inflexible preconceptions about how it ought to proceed. If changes in the Alliance should become necessary, this country's willingness to discuss them is a matter of record. Our basic objectives in Western Europe are simply to ensure the security of that area against aggression and to further its economic growth and political stability. On this point there certainly can be no disagreement between us and the European NATO partners.

Even on the most optimistic assumptions about the future, however, the Soviet Union will remain a great military power. We must expect that it will continue to probe for power vacuums, created by political or military weaknesses, into which it can project its political influence with only moderate risk to itself. Certainly the Soviet Union shows no sign of intending to reduce its own defense expenditures; on the contrary, it has increased them. Regardless of present intentions, a government with such great military power at its disposal can become hostile and dangerous overnight. Europe has obvious attractions to the Soviets, of course. After the United States, Western Europe today represents the greatest aggregation of economic, political and ideological strength in the world. The six Common Market nations, plus the United Kingdom, have by themselves a total population, military manpower pool and Gross National Product considerably larger than those of the Soviet Union. They have been able to provide their people with a much higher standard of living than that of the U.S.S.R. or any of its allies. There can be no question that Soviet domination of this area would be a grave threat to our own security. If the Western allies were ever to dismantle the effective military strength of the Alliance, or abandon its cohesive spirit and the cooperation of its military forces, they would create temptations for Soviet probings and adventures which nothing in Soviet history suggests it is prepared to withstand.

What we need to counterbalance the military capabilities of the Soviet Union and the Warsaw Pact countries is a full range of military strength which we can only secure and maintain by collective effort. The military role of NATO therefore will remain as necessary in the foreseeable future as it has been in the past. The progress that has been made in the relationships between East and West is due in large part to the West's having maintained a strong defense posture. Certainly this is no time to give it up.

On this matter we are in full agreement with thirteen other NATO members. The position of France is well known. In 1967 France withdrew her military forces from the unified NATO commands and set out to go her own way. At her request we and the other NATO allies withdrew our military forces from France, a move made with remarkable efficiency and at moderate cost. NATO Headquarters have now been relocated in Belgium and military units and supplies principally in the United Kingdom and the Federal Republic of Germany. Notwithstanding the impact of the French action, and I do not wish to minimize its importance, the unity of the fourteen members and the vitality of NATO as a military organization remain intact.

Indeed, a most significant step forward from the U.S. point of view was taken at the meeting of the NATO Council of Ministers in December, 1967. For the previous six years the United States had emphasized two major themes to its allies. The first was realism—the need to match NATO's strategic assumptions and plans with its *de facto* budgets and forces. The second was the need for a balance in NATO's and the Warsaw Pact's over-all capabilities. We argued that only the existence of a balanced force could convince an aggressor beyond doubt that whatever effort he might make—or perhaps even more important, threaten to make—would be matched by the Alliance. We emphasized that only under these conditions would it become obvious to the Soviet Union that military force of any kind or at any level would be useless as a means to secure political ends.

The principal subject of this debate was the proper response to levels of aggression below an unlimited strategic nuclear attack on our homelands. The discussion centered on the extent to which we should plan on the use of nuclear weapons as the main response to non-nuclear aggression. The United States has been firmly of the view that the threat of an incredible action is not an effective deterrent. The political leaders of the West are all well aware of the dangers involved in the use of tactical nuclear weapons, and so are the leaders of the Warsaw Pact nations. Soviet leaders probably would not believe that the nations of NATO would agree to run the great risk of using nuclear weapons to counter a limited form of political or military aggression. Therefore they might be tempted to probe or experiment with limited aggression in some crisis situations. They would hope to exploit possible differences among the NATO leaders in their assessments of the nuclear risks, and thus to achieve piecemeal what they could not accomplish by any sudden, massive, all-out attack on the Alliance.

Some NATO members have questioned the advisability of even discussing the U.S. view that nuclear forces are not a universal deterrent. It has been suggested that airing this view publicly would impair the deterrent. The answer to that is clear. First, it is both dangerous and deceptive to suppose that the Soviets are less intelligent than we, or that they would be disposed to believe in a bluff that we ourselves questioned. Second, experience has proven the contrary. Despite years of discussion of the appropriate deterrent and strategy against various forms of Soviet pressure and attack, the deterrent, in fact, has not been weakened. The Soviets have not been emboldened by our discussion to risk adventures against NATO. On the contrary, they appear to have understood clearly that it is not the American commitment to the defense of Europe that is in question, but only the most effective means of carrying it out.

I do not believe there is any doubt in the Soviet Union over the U.S. commitment to NATO. The simple fact is that the United States intends to continue its contribution to the forward defense of NATO with all the energy the task requires. It is our very readiness to keep this commitment which has led us, repeatedly, to urge NATO to develop the forces and the plans for times of need which would be acceptable to all the governments of the Alliance.

Now other members of the Alliance have acknowledged the need to plan for a broader range of contingencies than a massive attack against NATO launched with little warning. Much more remains to be done, both in the Alliance's Nuclear Planning Group of Defense Ministers and in the regular planning agencies of the Alliance. But the essential first step has been taken: a new political directive on strategy and forces has been adopted and a new force planning system has been created to carry it out.

In the meantime, the prime need of NATO continues to be greater flexibility in its force structure. It has now faced up to the importance of providing a full range of capabilities, rather than simply relying on the nuclear portion of its arsenal. Its main tasks for the future are the establishment of realistic goals for its forces and giving them sufficient flexibility, so we can adjust rapidly to preserve a balance of over-all military strength with the Warsaw Pact.

NATO will continue to need strong strategic nuclear forces, of course, and must retain an effective theater—or tactical—nuclear capability. We have already deployed a large number of nuclear weapons to Europe. This great theater capability should deter the Warsaw Pact from any attempt to seize Western Europe by an all-out conventional attack or by using its own tactical nuclear weapons.

As suggested earlier, however, the Alliance faces its

most challenging military problems, both for the short run and for the longer term, outside the nuclear field. Although there has been much improvement during the past seven years, NATO still does not have well-balanced conventional forces. There also are important qualitative deficiencies in the training, equipment and supplies of European NATO forces. Correction would bring the very greatest returns in effective combat strength for relatively modest additional expenditures. A still greater deficiency in the European NATO forces is the lack of an adequate mobilization base. The United States has made great progress in raising the combat readiness of its own reserve forces and in providing the means for their movement. It is most urgent that our European allies do likewise; the flexibility of NATO's force structure would be greatly improved.

This problem as to what constitutes adequate conventional forces stems in part from old misconceptions. Many Americans and Europeans, military and civilian, became accustomed years ago to the idea that the Warsaw Pact nations could overwhelm NATO's non-nuclear defenses in a surprise attack with nearly one hundred divisions against Germany alone. Even more devastating assaults, according to this assumption, could be opened with a minimum of warning. In the face of such expectations, the possibility of providing an adequate non-nuclear defense for NATO within realistic and acceptable defense budgets seemed hopeless.

When it was decided nonetheless in the early days of NATO to maintain substantial combat-ready ground forces, most members compromised. They provided nearly a million men in ready units, but economized on their training, equipment and supplies. Some countries allowed their mobilization bases to wither away in deference to the cost of their ready forces. Still, there was doubt that these ready forces could really cope with massive aggression from the Warsaw Pact. The alternatives for NATO, it was supposed, were either to give up territory and even accept defeat or to threaten the use of nuclear weapons from the very outset of an attack despite the risks of escalation. This misconception of the available choices developed in part from overestimates of Pact strength.

The Department of Defense in 1961 began to take a harder look at these estimates of the non-nuclear balance. We discovered that the actual size of the Soviet ground forces was substantially less than had been estimated previously. Their strength turned out to be closer to a million and a half than to two million men. Next, we recognized that large-scale surprise attacks by the Soviets were perhaps the least likely possibility in view of the poor readiness of many Soviet divisions. Now we can question whether massive attacks, without at least some warning, are feasible at all. It seems likely that the twenty-two small U.S.S.R. divisions in the Soviet Zone of Germany and Poland represent the only truly combat-ready Soviet divisions that could immediately threaten Central Europe. Using the same realistic assessments that we apply to our own forces, we believe that it would take weeks rather than days to reinforce them with the combat-ready and fully equipped units required for an all-out attack. Moreover, we are no longer convinced that the East European forces, which constitute more than half of the Warsaw Pact's combat-ready strength in Central Europe, would be fully effective in an unprovoked attack on NATO.

These considerations do not indicate that NATO now can match the mobilized strength of the Warsaw Pact armies, or that the Alliance can afford to relax its efforts. Rather, they suggest that we can achieve an important non-nuclear option in Europe at no higher cost, and perhaps at less cost, than we are now incurring. More precise assessment of our opponents' capabilities has made it clear that members of NATO can no longer contend that an impressive non-nuclear capability is beyond their reach. On the contrary, it is fully feasible.

On the whole, NATO already has the manpower in its active forces to deal with opposing combat units, even when East European divisions are counted. The deficiency is not in what we call M-day manpower—the forces available when mobilization is required. It lies rather in the need for improvement in deployment of NATO's forces in Germany, and the fact that not all of the supposedly combat-ready units are adequately trained, equipped and supplied. Conscription in many of the NATO countries is for eighteen months or less, and conscripts enter their M-day units with too little basic training. The ratio of support personnel to combat and combat-support personnel is frequently too low.

Once NATO's existing ready units are, in fact, combat-ready, our greatest need will be in mobilizable forces that will permit NATO clearly and demonstrably to keep pace with the Warsaw Pact in the deployment of reinforcements. This is particularly true in Central Europe. Even after we discount exaggerated estimates of the Warsaw Pact's deployment rate, the Soviets still possess a substantial capability for reinforcement. It is clear that NATO should have a better mobilization base from which to create counterweights against Soviet pressure. The European members of the Alliance will have to bear a realistic share of the burden.

The United States can more than double its combat-ready divisions in Central Europe within several weeks of mobilization. The Belgians, the Dutch, the British and the Canadians can provide a small number of units to this crucial area during the same period. It would appear that in an all-out race to deploy units, NATO could hold its own at various points along the way. We could still suffer a worrisome manpower disadvantage during at least one period of the competition, although not one which we should view as hopeless. This and other deficiencies can be corrected, and if NATO wants to make credibly clear to the Soviets that no threatened build-up will cause the Alliance to waver, it can do so. For the short run, this means NATO should maintain existing combat-ready ground forces and provide them with more extensive training, better equipment and larger stocks of combat consumables.

For the longer run, the United States has urged other

members to increase the number, training, supply and readiness level of their reserve divisions. The number required in Central Europe to match the Pact's capability is not beyond our reach, especially if U.S. reinforcements are counted as part of the total. Significantly, all the required reserve divisions, with their full equipment on hand, would cost no more than a few combat-ready divisions.

I am aware, of course, that the cost of maintaining combat-ready troops is substantial. Nonetheless, the defense efforts of some of our allies, measured against their overall economic strength, could well be increased. But even without increased defense expenditures a better allocation of resources within the Alliance would accomplish much of what I have been recommending.

NATO naval forces in some areas, for example, already exceed our needs. Several hundred million dollars might well be shifted to more urgently needed ground forces over the next five years. It may also prove possible to shift some resources from our air forces to ground-force improvements. Our NATO aircraft already have a good inherent non-nuclear capability and are qualitatively superior to those of the Warsaw Pact. The chief improvements we require are in modern ordnance, non-nuclear training for air and ground crews, and shelters to protect the aircraft from non-nuclear attack while on the ground.

Future expenditures on tactical air forces could thus be held to modest limits. Savings would be available here for improvements in ground forces, though, only if we avoid buying unnecessary follow-on aircraft that do not produce benefits to justify their higher costs.

Should NATO decide to adopt this realistic approach of balancing off Pact capabilities, what effects would it have on the posture and deployments of the Alliance? First, we would be keying the size and composition of our combat-ready forces to comparable, forward-deployed forces of the Warsaw Pact. Second, we would be setting mobilization and deployment schedules in accord with what the Pact, and specifically what the U.S.S.R., could do. Third, we would be introducing into our planning the kind of flexibility required by our new political guidance; that is, we would have plans both for different levels of mobilization and for the whole range of military contingencies. Fourth, while approximately the same over-all commitment of forces from members of the Alliance would still be necessary, the mix of on-the-line divisions, combat-ready deployable units and reserve forces could become much more flexible than it is today. As Pact deployments changed, so could ours.

The United States would expect to play a major role in supporting this approach. We would continue to maintain an adequate strategic nuclear deterrent for the Alliance as a whole; to keep sufficient tactical nuclear forces within the European theater; to deploy whatever U.S. air and ground forces were required on the ground in Europe for non-nuclear defense; and to keep available substantial reinforcements to supplement a European mobilization.

We recognize that our large military presence in Europe has acquired a particular symbolic importance in the eyes of some of our allies. Accordingly, we have continued to maintain in Europe for nearly twenty years powerful air and ground forces at a high state of readiness, as well as substantial Europe-oriented forces in the Continental United States, in order to give allies and potential enemies concrete evidence of our commitment to NATO.

I, for one, believe that the willingness of the United States to fulfill its obligations can no longer be in question, quite apart from the number of U.S. troops on the ground in Europe. I do not believe the Russians are in any doubt on this score. Therefore we should continue to maintain in Europe only those forces for which there is a clear military requirement.

In saying this, I must also point out an anomaly in European attitudes which we have discussed frankly with our allies. Some Europeans oppose any reduction in U.S. forces deployed in Europe, but at the same time disclaim responsibility for meeting the balance-of-payments deficit caused by such large-scale deployments. Such an anomaly cannot continue. Serious deficits suffered by countries as a direct result of stationing troops abroad in the common effort should be a matter of both concern and cooperative assistance on the part of their allies. We should welcome suggestions from them on how to meet this pressing problem, since its solution cannot be postponed.

In our planning we must also take greater account of changing technological, financial and military circumstances. There is, for one thing, the growing U.S. asset of strategic mobility. It will enable us soon to move forces from the Continental United States fast enough to match substantial build-ups by the Warsaw Pact. The Pact nations would be hard put to keep abreast if the European allies could mobilize and deploy—beyond existing levels—forces equal to those the United States could move to Europe in sixty days with its projected 1972 airlift capability. In other words, a large and rapid U.S. reinforcement should be taken into account in future NATO planning.

Some countries may feel that whatever the U.S. capability for strategic mobility, other commitments such as Vietnam, and the possibility that U.S. forces may become tied down in distant places, make these calculations and forecasts unrealistic. That sort of skepticism would be misplaced.

We understand very clearly, just as President Roosevelt did during World War II, that Europe has a primary claim on our military resources. By 1972 our strategic mobility will be such that we still could meet a very demanding schedule of deployments to Europe even if our forces were widely dispersed. U.S. strategic mobility, therefore, will be able in the foreseeable future to make a major new contribution to European defense of a kind hitherto associated only with forces permanently on the ground.

In my view, NATO has important military functions to perform for many years to come. I am convinced, however, that it can perform them satisfactorily only if it becomes more flexible, first in the means at its disposal and second in its plans for using them.

PART II

❖

The Tools of Power

CHAPTER FOUR

✳

Mutual Deterrence

IN a complex and uncertain world, the gravest problem that an American Secretary of Defense must face is that of planning, preparation and policy against the possibility of thermonuclear war. It is a prospect that most of mankind understandably would prefer not to contemplate, for technology has now circumscribed us all with a horizon of horror that could dwarf any catastrophe that has befallen man in his more than a million years on earth.

Man has lived now for more than twenty years in what we have come to call the Atomic Age. What we sometimes overlook is that every future age of man will be an atomic age, and if man is to have a future at all, it will have to be one overshadowed with the permanent possibility of thermonuclear holocaust. About that fact there is no longer any doubt. Our freedom in this question consists only in facing the matter rationally and realistically and discussing actions to minimize the danger.

No sane citizen, political leader or nation wants thermonuclear war. But merely not wanting it is not enough. We must understand the differences among actions which increase its risks, those which reduce them and those which, while costly, have little influence one way or another. But there is a great difficulty in the way of constructive and profitable debate over the issues, and that is the exceptional complexity of nuclear strategy. Unless these complexities are well understood, rational discussion and decision-making are impossible.

One must begin with precise definitions. The cornerstone of our strategic policy continues to be to deter deliberate nuclear attack upon the United States or its allies. We do this by maintaining a highly reliable ability to inflict unacceptable damage upon any single aggressor or combination of aggressors at any time during the course of a strategic nuclear exchange, even after absorbing a surprise first strike. This can be defined as our *assured-destruction capability*.

It is important to understand that assured destruction is the very essence of the whole deterrence concept. We must possess an actual assured-destruction capability, and that capability also must be credible. The point is that a potential aggressor must believe that our assured-destruction capability is in fact actual, and that our will to use it in retaliation to an attack is in fact unwavering. The conclusion, then, is clear: if the United States is to deter a nuclear attack on itself or its allies, it must possess an actual and a credible assured-destruction capability.

When calculating the force required, we must be conservative in all our estimates of both a potential aggressor's capabilities and his intentions. Security depends upon assuming a worst plausible case, and having the ability to cope with it. In that eventuality we must be able to absorb the total weight of nuclear attack on our country—on our retaliatory forces, on our command and control apparatus, on our industrial capacity, on our cities, and on our population—and still be capable of damaging the aggressor to the point that his society would be simply no longer viable in twentieth-century terms. That is what deterrence of nuclear aggression means. It means the certainty of suicide to the aggressor, not merely to his military forces, but to his society as a whole.

Let us consider another term: *first-strike capability*. This is a somewhat ambiguous term, since it could mean simply the ability of one nation to attack another nation with nuclear forces first. But as it is normally used, it connotes much more: the elimination of the attacked nation's retaliatory second-strike forces. This is the sense in which it should be understood.

Clearly, first-strike capability is an important strategic concept. The United States must not and will not permit itself ever to get into a position in which another nation, or combination of nations, would possess a first-strike capability against it. Such a position not only would constitute an intolerable threat to our security, but it obviously would remove our ability to deter nuclear aggression.

We are not in that position today, and there is no foreseeable danger of our ever getting into that position. Our strategic offensive forces are immense: 1,000 Minuteman missile launchers, carefully protected belowground; 41 Polaris submarines, carrying 656 missile launchers, with the majority hidden beneath the seas at all times; and about 600 long-range bombers, approximately 40 percent of which are kept always in a high state of alert.

Our alert forces alone carry more than 2,200 weapons, each averaging more than the explosive equivalent of one megaton of TNT. Four hundred of these delivered on the Soviet Union would be sufficient to destroy over one-third of her population and one-half of her industry. All these flexible and highly reliable forces are equipped with devices that ensure their penetration of Soviet defenses.

Now what about the Soviet Union? Does it today possess a powerful nuclear arsenal? The answer is that it does. Does it possess a first-strike capability against the United States? The answer is that it does not. Can the Soviet Union in the foreseeable future acquire such a first-strike capability against the United States? The answer is that it cannot. It cannot because we are determined to remain fully alert and we will never permit our own assured-destruction capability to drop to a point at which a Soviet first-strike capability is even remotely feasible.

Is the Soviet Union seriously attempting to acquire a first-strike capability against the United States? Although this is a question we cannot answer with absolute certainty, we believe the answer is no. In any event, the question itself is —in a sense—irrelevant; for the United States will maintain and, where necessary, strengthen its retaliatory forces so that, whatever the Soviet Union's intentions or actions, we will continue to have an assured-destruction capability vis-à-vis their society.

But there is another question that is most relevant. Does the United States, then, possess a first-strike capability against the Soviet Union? The answer is that we do not. We do not have this capability, not because we have neglected our nuclear strength; on the contrary, we have increased it to the point that we possess a clear superiority over the Soviet Union. We do not possess first-strike capability against the Soviet Union for precisely the same reason that they do not possess it against us. Quite simply, we have both built up our second-strike capability—in effect, retaliatory power—to the point that a first-strike capability on either side has become unattainable.

There is, of course, no way by which the United States could have prevented the Soviet Union from acquiring its present second-strike capability, short of a massive pre-emptive first strike in the 1950s. The fact is, then, that neither the Soviet Union nor the United States can attack the other without being destroyed in retaliation; nor can either of us attain a first-strike capability in the foreseeable future. Further, both the Soviet Union and the United

States now possess an actual and credible second-strike capability against one another, and it is precisely this mutual capability that provides us both with the strongest possible motive to avoid a nuclear war.

The most frequent question that arises in this connection is whether or not the United States possesses nuclear superiority over the Soviet Union. The answer is that we do.

But the answer, like everything else in this matter, is technically complex. The complexity arises in part out of what measurement of superiority is most meaningful and realistic. Many commentators on the matter tend to define nuclear superiority in terms of gross megatonnage, or in terms of the number of missile launchers available. By both these standards the United States does have a substantial superiority over the Soviet Union in the weapons targeted against each other. But it is precisely these two standards of measurement that are themselves misleading. Instead, the most meaningful and realistic measurement of nuclear capability is the number of separate warheads that can be delivered accurately on individual high-priority targets with sufficient power to destroy them.

Gross megatonnage alone is an inadequate indicator of assured-destruction capability since it is unrelated to survivability, accuracy or penetrability, and poorly related to effective elimination of multiple high-priority targets. There obviously is no advantage in overdestroying one target at the expense of leaving undamaged other targets of equal importance. Further, the number of missile launchers available is also an inadequate indicator of assured-destruction capability since many of our launchers will carry multiple warheads.

But using the realistic measurement of the number of warheads available, those which could be delivered with accuracy and effectiveness on appropriate targets in the United States or Soviet Union, the United States currently possesses a superiority over the Soviet Union of at least three or four to one. Furthermore, we will maintain superiority by these same realistic criteria for as far ahead as we can realistically plan.

One point should be made quite clear, however: our current numerical superiority over the Soviet Union in reliable, accurate and effective warheads is both greater than we had originally planned and more than we require. In the larger equation of security our superiority is of limited significance, for even with our current superiority, or indeed with any numerical superiority realistically attainable, the blunt, inescapable fact remains that the Soviet Union, with its present forces, could still effectively destroy the United States, even after absorbing the full weight of an American first strike.

I have noted that our present superiority is greater than we had planned. How this came about is a significant illustration of the intrinsic dynamics of the nuclear arms race.

In 1961 when I became Secretary of Defense, the Soviet Union had a very small operational arsenal of intercontinental missiles. However, it did possess the technological and industrial capacity to enlarge that arsenal very substantially over the succeeding several years. We had no evidence that the Soviets did plan, in fact, fully to use that capability. But, as I have pointed out, a strategic planner must be conservative in his calculations; that is, he must prepare for the worst plausible case and not be content to hope and prepare merely for the most probable.

Since we could not be certain of Soviet intentions, since we could not be sure that they would not undertake a massive build-up, we had to insure against such an eventuality by undertaking a major build-up of our own Minuteman and Polaris forces. Thus, in the course of hedging against what was then only a theoretically possible Soviet build-up, we took decisions which have resulted in our current superiority in numbers of warheads and deliverable megatons. But the blunt fact remains that if we had had more accurate information about planned Soviet strategic forces, we simply would not have needed to build as large a nuclear arsenal as we have today.

Let me be absolutely clear. I am not saying that our decision in 1961 was unjustified; I am saying that it was necessitated by a lack of accurate information. Furthermore, that decision in itself, justified as it was, in the end could not possibly have left unaffected the Soviet Union's future nuclear plans.

What is essential to understand here is that the Soviet Union and the United States mutually influence one another's strategic plans. Whatever their intentions or our intentions, actions—or even realistically potential actions—on either side relating to the build-up of nuclear forces necessarily trigger reactions on the other side. It is precisely this action-reaction phenomenon that fuels an arms race.

In strategic nuclear weaponry the arms race involves a particular irony. Unlike any other era in military history, a substantial numerical superiority of weapons today does not effectively translate into political control or diplomatic leverage. While thermonuclear power is almost inconceivably awesome and represents virtually unlimited potential destructiveness, it has proven to be a limited diplomatic instrument. Its uniqueness lies in the fact that it is at the same time an all-powerful weapon and a very inadequate weapon.

The fact that the Soviet Union and the United States can mutually destroy one another regardless of who strikes first narrows the range of Soviet aggression which our nuclear forces can effectively deter. Even with our nuclear monopoly in the early postwar period, we were unable to deter the Soviet pressures against Berlin or their support of aggression in Korea. Today our nuclear superiority does not deter all forms of Soviet support of Communist insurgency in Southeast Asia. What all of this has meant is that we, and our allies as well, require substantial non-nuclear forces in order to cope with levels of aggression that massive strategic forces do not, in fact, deter.

This has been a difficult lesson both for us and for our allies to accept. There is a strong psychological tendency to regard superior nuclear forces as a simple and unfailing solution to security and an assurance of victory under any set of circumstances. What must be understood is that our

nuclear strategic forces play a vital and absolutely necessary role in our security and that of our allies, but it is an
intrinsically limited role. Therefore we and our allies must
maintain substantial conventional forces, fully capable of
dealing with a wide spectrum of lesser forms of political
and military aggression. This is a level of aggression against
which the use of strategic nuclear forces would not be to
our advantage, and thus a level of aggression which these
strategic nuclear forces by themselves cannot effectively
deter. One cannot fashion a credible deterrent out of an
incredible action. Thus security for the United States and
its allies can only arise from the possession of a range of
graduated deterrents, each of them fully credible in its
own context.

In recent years the Soviets have substantially increased
their offensive forces. We have been watching and evalu-
ating this very carefully, of course; clearly the Soviet
build-up is in part a reaction to our own build-up since the
beginning of the 1960s. Soviet strategic planners undoubtedly reasoned that if our build-up were to continue at
its accelerated pace, we might conceivably reach in time a
credible first-strike capability against the Soviet Union.

That was not, in fact, our intention. Our goal was to
ensure that they, with their theoretical capacity to reach
such a first-strike capability, would not outdistance us. But
they could not read our intentions with any greater accuracy than we could read theirs. The result has been that
we have both built up our forces to a point that far exceeds
a credible second-strike capability against the forces we
each started with. In doing so neither of us has reached a

first-strike capability. And the realities of the situation being what they are—whatever we believe their intentions to be, and whatever they believe our intentions to be—each of us can deny the other a first-strike capability in the foreseeable future.

How can we be so confident that this is the case? How can we be so certain that the Soviets cannot gradually outdistance us, either by some dramatic technological breakthrough or simply through our imperceptibly lagging behind, for whatever reason: reluctance to spend the requisite funds, distraction with military problems elsewhere, faulty intelligence, or simple negligence and naïveté? All of these reasons and others have been suggested by some commentators in this country who fear that we are, in fact, falling behind to a dangerous degree.

The answer is simple and straightforward. We are not going to permit the Soviets to outdistance us, because to do so would be to jeopardize our very viability as a nation. No President, no Secretary of Defense, no Congress of the United States of whatever political persuasion is going to permit this nation to take that risk. We do not want a nuclear arms race with the Soviet Union, primarily because the action-reaction phenomenon makes it foolish and futile. But if the only way to prevent the Soviet Union from obtaining first-strike capability over us is to engage in such a race, the United States possesses in ample abundance the resources, the technology and the will to run faster in that race for whatever distance is required.

What we would much prefer to do is to come to a realistic and reasonably riskless agreement with the Soviet

Union which would effectively prevent such an arms race. We both have strategic nuclear arsenals greatly in excess of a credible assured-destruction capability. These arsenals have reached that point of excess in each case for precisely the same reason: we each have reacted to the other's build-up with very conservative calculations. We have, that is, each built a greater arsenal than either of us needed for a second-strike capability, simply because both wanted to be able to cope with the worst plausible case.

Since we each now possess a deterrent in excess of our individual needs, both of our nations would benefit from a properly safeguarded agreement first to limit and later to reduce both our offensive and defensive strategic nuclear forces. We believe such an agreement is fully feasible since it is clearly in the interests of both our nations. But formal agreement or not, we can be sure that neither the Soviets nor we are going to risk the other's obtaining a first-strike capability. On the contrary, we can be sure that we are both going to maintain a maximum effort to preserve an assured-destruction capability.

It would not be sensible for either side to launch a maximum effort to achieve a first-strike capability. The intelligence-gathering capability of each side being what it is, and the realities of lead-time from technological breakthrough to operational readiness being what they are, neither of us would be able to acquire a first-strike capability in secret.

Now let me take a specific case in point. The Soviets are now deploying an antiballistic-missile system. If we react to this deployment intelligently, we have no reason for alarm. The system does not impose any threat to our ability to penetrate and inflict massive and unacceptable damage on the Soviet Union. In other words, it does not now affect in any significant manner our assured-destruction capability. It does not impose a threat because we have already taken the steps necessary to assure that our land-based Minuteman missiles, our submarine-launched new Poseidon missiles and our strategic bomber forces have the necessary penetration aids. They constitute a force of great magnitude, strong enough to survive a Soviet attack and penetrate the Soviet ABM deployment.

Now let us consider an issue that has received much attention recently: the question of whether or not we should deploy an ABM system against the Soviet nuclear threat.* To begin with, this is not in any sense a new issue. We have had both the technical possibility and the strategic desirability of an American ABM deployment under constant review since the late 1950s. While we have substantially improved our technology in the field, it is important to understand that none of the systems at the present or fore-seeable state of the art would provide an impenetrable shield over the United States. Were such a shield possible, we would certainly want it and we would certainly build it.

At this point, let me dispose of an objection that is totally irrelevant to this issue. It has been alleged that we are opposed to deploying a large-scale ABM system because it would carry the heavy price tag of $40 billion. Let me make it very clear that the $40 billion is not the issue. If we could

* Appendix I describes other threats against which an ABM system might be deployed.

build and deploy a genuinely impenetrable shield over the United States, we would be willing to spend not only $40 billion, but any reasonable multiple of that amount that was necessary. The money in itself is not the problem; the penetrability of the proposed shield is the problem.

There is clearly no point in spending $40 billion if it is not going to buy us a significant improvement in our security. If it is not, then we should use the substantial resources it represents on something that will. Every ABM system that is now feasible involves firing defensive missiles at incoming offensive warheads in an effort to destroy them. What many commentators on this issue overlook is that any such system can rather obviously be defeated by an enemy's simply sending more offensive warheads, or dummy warheads, than there are defensive missiles capable of disposing of them. This is the crux of the nuclear action-reaction phenomenon. Were we to deploy a heavy ABM system throughout the United States, the Soviets would clearly be strongly motivated to so increase their offensive capability as to cancel out our defensive advantage.

It is futile for each of us to spend $4 billion, $40 billion or $400 billion—and, at the end of all the spending, at the end of all the deployment, at the end of all the effort, to be relatively at the same point of balance on the security scale that we are now. Actually, we have already initiated offensive-weapons programs costing several billions in order to offset the small present Soviet ABM deployment, and the possibly more extensive future Soviet ABM deployments. That is money well spent, and it is necessary.

We should bear in mind, however, that it is money spent because of the action-reaction phenomenon. If we in turn opt for heavy ABM deployment, at whatever price, we can be certain that the Soviets will react to offset the advantage we would hope to gain.

It is precisely because of this certainty of a corresponding Soviet reaction that the four prominent scientists who have served with distinction as the Science Advisers to Presidents Eisenhower, Kennedy and Johnson, and the three outstanding men who have served as Directors of Research and Engineering to three Secretaries of Defense, have unanimously recommended against the deployment of an ABM system.

But the plain fact of the matter is that we are now facing a situation analogous to the one we faced in 1961: we are uncertain of the Soviets' intentions. At that time we were concerned about their potential offensive capabilities; now we are concerned about their potential defensive capabilities. The dynamics of the concern are the same. We must continue to be cautious and conservative in our estimates, leaving no room in our calculations for unnecessary risk. And at the same time, we must measure our own response in such a manner that it does not trigger a senseless spiral upward of nuclear arms.

As I have emphasized, we have already taken the necessary steps to guarantee that our offensive strategic weapons will be able to penetrate future, more advanced Soviet defenses. Keeping in mind the careful clockwork of lead-time, we will be forced to continue that effort over the next few years if the evidence is that the Soviets intend to turn what is now a light and modest ABM deployment into a massive one. Should they elect to do so, we have both the lead-time and the technology available to increase both the quality and the quantity of our offensive strategic forces, with particular attention to highly reliable penetration aids, so that their defensive efforts will give them no edge whatever in the nuclear balance.

We would prefer not to have to do that, however. It is a profitless waste of resources, provided we and the Soviets can come to a realistic strategic arms-limitation agreement. We proposed U.S.-Soviet talks on this matter. Should this effort fail, we are fully prepared to take the appropriate measures that such a failure would make necessary.

The point to keep in mind, however, is that if the talks do fail, and the Soviets decide to expand their ABM deployment, our response must be realistic. There is no point whatever in our responding by going to a massive ABM deployment to protect our population when such a system would be ineffective against a sophisticated Soviet offense. Instead, realism dictates that we then must further expand our sophisticated offensive forces and thus preserve our overwhelming assured-destruction capability. The intractable fact is that both the Soviets and we would be forced to continue on a foolish and unproductive course. In the end it would provide neither the Soviets nor us with any greater relative nuclear capability. The time has come for us both to realize that and to act reasonably. It is clearly in our own mutual interest to do so.

The road leading from the stone age to the ICBM, though

it may have been more than a million years in the building, seems to have run in a single direction. If one is inclined to be cynical, one might conclude that man's history seems to be characterized not so much by consistent periods of peace, occasionally punctuated by warfare, as by persistent outbreaks of warfare, wearily put aside from time to time for periods of exhaustion and recovery that parade under the name of peace.

I do not view man's history with that degree of cynicism, but I do believe that man's wisdom in avoiding war is often surpassed by his folly in promoting it. However foolish unlimited war may have been in the past, it is now no longer merely foolish, but suicidal as well. It is said that nothing can prevent a man from suicide if he is sufficiently determined to commit it. The question is: what is our determination in an era when unlimited war will mean the death of hundreds of millions and the possible genetic impairment of a million generations to follow?

Man is clearly a compound of folly and wisdom, and history is clearly a consequence of the admixture of those two contradictory traits. History has placed our particular lives in an era when the consequences of human folly are waxing more and more catastrophic in the matters of war and peace. In the end, the root of man's security does not lie in his weaponry, it lies in his mind. What the world requires in its third decade of the Atomic Age is not a new race toward armament, but a new race toward reasonableness.

We had all better run that race.

CHAPTER FIVE

✳

The Choice of Weapons

UP to this point I have spoken of weapons and men under arms in terms secondary to policy: our place in the world and the limits which the very appearance of nuclear weapons imposed on the exercise of power. Superior weapons are essential for survival in today's world, but I do not believe they guarantee our long-range security—a point I intend to make in detail later. Yet certainly if Americans are to debate intelligently the issues in world affairs, as I believe they must, they need to understand their government's decisions on military strength and the forces those decisions produced.

When I entered the Defense Department in 1961, several basic considerations were becoming clear. We had to improve our strategic nuclear forces even as we fit them into our new understanding of their place in the balance of power, and we had to increase greatly the emphasis on our conventional forces. There seemed to be a consensus on this general need for improvement in both areas, though from time to time there was brisk debate over the specific measures to achieve it.

One of the first things we had to do was to separate the problem of strategic nuclear war from all other kinds of war. Careful analysis revealed two important facts on this point: One was that strategic nuclear forces in themselves no longer constituted a credible deterrent to the broad range of aggression, if indeed they ever had in the past. The other was that we could not substitute tactical nuclear weapons for conventional forces in the types of conflicts that were most likely to involve us in the period of the 1960s.

We agreed, of course, that an effective tactical nuclear capability was essential to our over-all strategy. But we also felt very strongly that the decision to employ such nuclear weapons should not be forced upon us simply because we had no other means to cope with conflict. We recognized then what has become so obvious now, that there would inevitably be many situations in which it would be neither feasible nor advisable to use tactical nuclear weapons. Hence, what we sought to achieve was a greater degree of versatility in our general-purpose forces.

This is not to say that consideration of the general nuclear war problem had been overlooked prior to 1961, nor did I and my associates clearly understand or even perceive all of the aspects of this vastly complex problem from the very outset. Quite the contrary; many of the fundamental concepts and insights which underlie our nuclear policies and programs today were developed prior to 1961, and my own views have matured and become more precise since that time. Indeed, many of the issues which came to a head in 1961 had been debated for years. All needed to be resolved so that we could get on with the job of reshaping our strategy and our forces for the decade of the 1960s. We still had to face squarely the fact that strategic nuclear forces, no matter how versatile and powerful, do not by themselves constitute a credible deterrent to all kinds of aggression.

There was, of course, a deep and vivid awareness from the very beginning of the nuclear era that a war in which large numbers of atomic bombs were employed would be far different from any ever fought before. In such a war the potential battlefield would be the entire homelands of the participants. Throughout the 1950s, and indeed since the end of World War II, it had always been our capacity to retaliate with massive nuclear power which was considered to be the deterrent against Soviet attack. It was this tendency to rely on nuclear weapons as the universal deterrent that helped contribute to the decline in our non-nuclear limited-war forces, first during the late 1940s and then during the second half of the 1950s. By 1961 it was becoming clear that large-scale use of nuclear weapons by the West as a response to Soviet aggression, other than an unlimited attack, was not desirable. Therefore other types of forces would have to be provided both to deter and, in the event deterrence failed, to cope with conflicts at the middle and lower end of the spectrum.

Thus the time was ripe for a general reassessment of our military forces in relation to our national security policies and objectives. With regard to our strategic nuclear war capabilities, our initial analysis impressed us with the need for prompt action in three related areas. First, our strategic offensive forces were then fully adequate for their mission, but it was apparent that our relatively unprotected missiles and bombers would become exceedingly vulnerable to a nuclear surprise attack once our opponent had acquired a large number of operational intercontinental ballistic missiles (ICBMs). Second, when that threat became a reality, reliable warning and quick response to warning of a missile attack would be crucial to the survival of our bomber forces. Third, improvements would have to be made in our command and communications systems if the strategic offensive forces were to be kept continuously under the control of the constituted authorities—before, during and after a nuclear attack.

There appeared to be two basic approaches available to us at the time: (1) we could provide offensive forces to be launched quickly after warning from the Ballistic Missile Early Warning System, which was then still under construction; or (2) we could provide forces able to survive a massive ICBM attack and then be launched in retaliation. As a long-term solution, the first approach was rejected because of its great dependence on timely and unambiguous warning. In the case of the manned bombers, this uncertainty presented serious but not necessarily critical problems. The bombers could be launched upon warning and ordered to proceed to their targets only after the evidence of an attack was unmistakable. But once launched a ballistic missile could not be recalled. Yet unless it was deployed in a form which gave it a good chance of surviving an attack, it too would have to be launched before the enemy's missiles struck home.

Obviously, it would be extremely dangerous for everyone if we were to rely on a deterrent missile force whose survival depended on a hair-trigger response to the first indications of an attack. Accordingly, we decided to accelerate the shift from the first-generation ICBMs, the liquid-fuel Atlas and Titan, to the second-generation solid-fuel missiles, Polaris and Minuteman. The former types were very costly and difficult to deploy in hardened underground sites and maintain on a suitable alert status. We knew that the Minuteman would not only be less expensive to produce and deploy in protected sites, but would also be considerably easier and less costly to keep on alert. Because of its unique launching platform, the submarine-carried Polaris missile inherently promised a high likelihood of surviving a surprise attack.

As these more survivable and effective Polaris and Minuteman missiles entered the operational forces in large numbers during 1964-65, the older Regulus, Atlas and Titan I types were phased out. And over the years as advancing technology produced new models of the Minuteman and Polaris—"models" which represented as great an advance over their predecessors as the B-52 over the B-47 —these too were promptly introduced. Finally, a very large missile-penetration-aids effort was undertaken to make certain that we could overcome any enemy defensive measures designed to stop our missiles. Despite the retirement of all the Atlases and Titan I's, the number of land-based ICBMs increased from 28 at mid-1961 to 1,054 by mid-1967. All the planned 41 Polaris submarines have now become operational, most with advanced-model Polaris missiles.

With regard to the manned bombers, it was clearly evident in 1961 that the number that could be maintained on alert status was far more important than the total in the inventory. Until the Minuteman and Polaris forces could be deployed, we increased by 50 percent the proportion of the force maintained on fifteen-minute ground alert, the warning time we could expect from our Early Warning System.

The increase in the strategic bomber force to fourteen wings of B-52s and two wings of B-58s was completed in 1963. During this same period the force of older B-47 medium bombers was phased down, eventually being retired completely in 1966 on essentially the same schedule planned by the previous Administration. In addition, a large and very expensive B-52 modification program was undertaken. Our goal was to extend the useful life of the later models well into the 1970s and enable them to employ low-altitude tactics to improve their penetration capabilities against enemy defenses.

As a result of these changes, the number of nuclear weapons in the alert force increased over threefold during the period. Now that the Minuteman and Polaris forces had been deployed, we first reduced and finally eliminated the bomber airborne alert. As the weight of the threat continued to shift from bombers to missiles, we began to modify the air-defense system, phasing out those elements which became obsolete or in excess of our needs.

We also closely considered in 1961 the advisability of deploying an active defense against ballistic-missile attack. However, there were widespread doubts even then as to whether the Nike-Zeus system, which had been under development since 1956, should ever be deployed. Weighing all the pros and cons, we concluded in 1962 that the best course was to shift development of the system to a more advanced approach and take no action to produce and deploy it at that time. We then stepped up our exploration of the entire problem of detecting, tracking, intercepting and destroying ballistic missiles. It was from these efforts that we have since drawn much of the technology incorporated in our present ballistic-missile defense concepts.

Finally, we undertook an extensive program to improve and make more secure the command and control of our strategic offensive forces. Among the measures was the establishment of alternate national command centers. These included some which would be maintained continuously in the air so that the direction of all our forces would not have to depend upon the survival of a single center. Steps taken to improve the various command and communications systems included, for example, provision for the airborne control of bomber, Minuteman and Polaris launchings. These were all forged into a new integrated National Military Command System.

Many of the tasks we set for ourselves seven years ago have been successfully accomplished. But the situation which we foresaw then is now well upon us. The Soviets have, in fact, acquired a large force of ICBMs installed in hardened underground silos. As the previous chapter emphasized, neither the Soviet Union nor the United States can now attack the other, even by complete surprise, without suffering massive damage in retaliation. Each side has achieved, and will most likely maintain over the foreseeable future, an actual and credible second-strike capability against the other. It is precisely this mutual capability to destroy one another and, conversely, our respective inability to prevent such destruction that provide us both with the strongest possible motive to avoid a strategic nuclear war. The prospect that China eventually may acquire a credible strategic nuclear system is adding a new dimension to these fundamental considerations, of course. It is an element constantly in the minds of those charged with projecting the political and military means of our safety and survival in the years ahead.

I believe we can all agree that the cornerstone of our strategic policy must continue to be the deterrence of a deliberate nuclear attack against the United States or its allies. From that cornerstone, we must answer the specific question: What level of potential destruction would have to be achieved to maintain that deterrence? A corollary to the answer, without which it would be meaningless, is that it would have to be understood fully by potential adversaries.

Some people have argued that the Soviet or Red Chinese tolerance of damage would be much higher than our own. Even if this were true—which is debatable—it would simply mean that we must maintain a greater assured-destruction capability. In the case of the Soviet Union, I would judge that a capability on our part to destroy, say, one-fifth to one-fourth of her population and one-half of her industrial capacity would serve as an effective deterrent. Such a level of destruction would certainly represent intolerable punishment to any twentieth-century industrial nation.

Mainland China represents a somewhat different problem. Today she is still far from being an industrial nation. What industry she has is heavily concentrated in a comparatively few cities. We estimate, for example, that a relatively small number of warheads would destroy the majority of her industrial capacity. Such an attack also would destroy most of the key governmental structures and communications facilities. Since China's capacity to attack the United States with nuclear weapons will be very limited at least through the 1970s, the ability of even so small a portion of our strategic forces to inflict such heavy damage upon them should serve as a major deterrent to a deliberate attack on the United States.

The next question which has to be answered is: what kind and how large a force do we need to ensure that we can inflict the necessary level of damage on the attacker? The requirement for assured-destruction forces can be determined logically only by the size and character of the target system, taking account of all the other relevant factors. Among these are the number of our weapons which at any given time are ready to be launched toward their target; the number which could be expected to survive a Soviet surprise first attack; and the number of the "ready," surviving weapons which can reasonably be expected to reach the objective area, survive enemy defenses and strike their intended targets.

Thus a logical determination of strategic-force requirements involves a rather complex set of calculations. Obviously a change in any major element of the problem necessitates changes in many other elements. For example, the Soviet deployment of a very extensive air-defense system during the 1950s forced us to make some very important changes in our strategic bomber forces. The B-52s had to be provided with penetration aids, such as standoff missiles, decoys and electronic countermeasure equipment. In addition, the B-52 airframe had to be substantially strengthened to permit sustained low-altitude operations.

Now, in the late 1960s, because the Soviet Union might deploy extensive antimissile defenses, we are making some very important changes in our strategic missile forces.

Instead of a single large warhead, our missiles are now being designed to carry several small warheads and penetrations aids. It is the number of warheads, or objects which *appear* to be warheads to the defender's radars, that will determine the outcome in a contest with an ABM defense.

All of these considerations, illustrating both the strengths and limitations of nuclear weapons, had an immediate corollary in the obvious need for improvement in our nonnuclear capability. Consequently we gave our conventional forces early and high priority in 1961. Our preliminary evaluation convinced us that we and our allies would have to make a much greater effort toward a force structure which could cope with limited aggression. The threat was clear when measured against the relatively reduced state of our conventional forces: we might have to face tests ranging from small-scale guerrilla and subversive activities to overt attacks by sizable military units. We concluded that we would have to improve organization, manning, equipment, training, mobility and, most especially, the balance among all elements of the forces.

As a start we increased the purchase of conventional weapons, ammunition and equipment, expanded the Navy's ship-maintenance program, ordered construction of more amphibious transports, and modified Air Force tactical fighters to improve their non-nuclear delivery capability. In addition, we stepped up the pace of training; began revamping the Army reserves; added personnel to the Army and its Special Forces, as well as the Marine Corps and its

Reserve; increased airlift capability; and intensified non-nuclear military research and development.

These first steps were overtaken by the Berlin crisis. The need to call up Reserves during that period confirmed our belief that much more fundamental changes would have to be made if our general-purpose forces were to meet our long-range objectives. But deciding how best to strengthen our limited-war capabilities is greatly complicated by several factors. They include the wide variety of war contingencies for which we must be prepared; the sheer numbers and kinds of units, weapons, equipment and supplies involved; the important role Reserves play in these forces; and, finally, the derivative relationship between our own requirements and those of our allies.

The over-all requirement for general-purpose forces is related not so much to the defense of our own territory, of course, as it is to the support of our commitments to other nations. Each of these commitments gives rise to contingencies for which we must plan. This does not mean that we will ever be confronted by forty-odd South Vietnams simultaneously, however. These commitments do not require us to execute automatically any specific contingency plan in response to a given situation, without regard to the circumstances existing at the time. And while we cannot expect to meet all the contingencies simultaneously, neither can our opponents. Our policy has been to set the size of the general-purpose forces so that we can simultaneously meet the more probable contingencies.

The largest contingency outside NATO, in terms of potential U.S. force requirements, is a Chinese attack on Southeast Asia. Therefore we had to provide, in addition to our NATO requirements, the forces required to meet such an attack in Asia as well as to fulfill our commitments in the Western Hemisphere. Because of the basic uncertainty inherent in estimates of such requirements, we then added to these force requirements provisions for a Strategic Reserve.

I should emphasize that we have considerable flexibility in meeting other possible contingencies which require smaller forces, or those not requiring so rapid a build-up. For example, in the Vietnam conflict we used the forces earmarked for a major Asian contingency to meet the immediate needs in the summer of 1965 and then activated temporary forces to meet the longer-range needs. The very stability of our own NATO contribution during that period is a significant example of the flexibility we developed.

More generally, NATO forces in the North Atlantic area are about equal in manpower to those of the Warsaw Pact in all regions except the Far North. NATO has about 900,000 troops deployed in all regions on Continental Europe, compared to 960,000 troops for the Warsaw Pact. While manpower comparisons alone are not conclusive measures of military strength, I believe they are reasonable first approximations of relative ground forces. Moreover, our relative air capability is far greater than a simple comparison of numbers would indicate. By almost every measure

NATO (especially U.S.) air forces are superior to those of the Warsaw Pact for non-nuclear war.

If either side chose, the ready land forces could be greatly reinforced before any fighting began, as in the 1961 Berlin crisis. Assuming a simultaneous mobilization, within thirty days the Pact would probably gain a manpower advantage on the Central front and a somewhat greater advantage in over-all ground-combat capability. This gap would then begin to narrow with the arrival of still more U.S. forces.

NATO tactical aircraft reinforcements would about equal the Pact's in the early stages of mobilization, after which we could add considerably more. Our main advantage in this area, however, stems from the great superiority of our aircraft, pilots and weapons. In my judgment, the forces planned are adequate to meet our objectives, especially if our allies make the improvements proposed in the earlier consideration of NATO.

The most likely kind of conflict in NATO Europe is one arising from miscalculation during a period of tension, rather than a deliberately preplanned Soviet attack. But we cannot entirely discount such a deliberate attack. If the Soviets were to attack following a successful concealed mobilization, they could have, temporarily, a substantial advantage in land forces. Our own forces are large enough, however, to require them to build up and attack with a huge force. Such a mobilization would be, at best, difficult to hide. In any event, the Soviet Union and her East European allies would have to assume that the West might react against such an attack with nuclear weapons. Considering the destructive potential of both our theater and strategic nuclear forces, and the fact that a deliberate attack would constitute a clear threat to our vital interests, the Soviets should be strongly deterred from attempting this strategy.

In keeping with these considerations our non-nuclear forces grew rapidly in the years following 1961. The number of active combat-assigned Army divisions was increased from eleven to sixteen as we added the men to fill them out and sustain the training base that would keep them up to strength. The total number of combat-assigned divisions— Army and Marine, active and Reserve—in the permanent force was increased by 66 percent.

The procurement of conventional weapons and support systems was greatly expanded. For example, during 1962-65 direct obligations for Army procurement were about 60 percent greater than during the previous four years. In addition, the Army reorganized its divisions, dropping the nuclear-oriented pentomic configuration and introducing its ROAD concept. What the reorganization did, essentially, was fix the framework for a quick shift of forces to meet a variety of combat situations. It also laid the organizational groundwork for needed increases in firepower and mobility.

The number of active and reserve mechanized Army infantry and tank units was increased by 110 percent, and their tanks and tactical vehicles were modernized. Much improved mobility, especially for our forces oriented toward underdeveloped areas, was obtained through greater emphasis on helicopters. In 1961 the Army and Marine Corps had about 3,100 helicopters, all but 200 of which had piston engines. By the end of fiscal 1970, when 1968 orders will be delivered, we will have about 7,500 modern turbine helicopters, with much greater capacity and speed and higher possible utilization rates than the ones they replaced.

New air-mobility concepts were introduced into land-force operations. The creation of a provisional air-assault division permitted us to test air-mobility concepts in 1964-65, and allowed us to form the first Airmobile Division in time to deploy it to Southeast Asia in the summer of 1965.

The United States has about 7,000 tactical aircraft, and its allies have another 6,000, about the same number as were available in 1961, and about the same as the current world-wide Communist total. At the same time, our tactical air *capability* has increased dramatically, relative both to 1961 and to the threat. Under our presently planned program this trend will continue through the early 1970s. This increase in over-all capability results from modernization of forces together with major improvements in conventional ordnance. For instance, we have doubled the payload of our tactical aircraft since 1961, and we will double it again by 1972.

Of all the thousands of changes made in our military forces over the seven-year period, the single area of strategic movement comes closest to illustrating how we tried to meet the new demands on non-nuclear capability. The central question here, of course, is the ability to move quickly to meet possible threats, conceivably at widely separated points in the world. There are essentially two main approaches. The first is to maintain very large conventional forces stationed around the globe near all potential trouble spots. The second is to maintain a smaller central reserve of highly ready forces, supported by the means to move them promptly wherever they might be needed. These two approaches have never been truly distinct alternatives, but both the relative feasibility and desirability of the second have greatly increased during the last decade.

The most obvious and pressing requirement in early 1961 was for greatly improved strategic airlift. Our early actions included a step-up in the C-130 program, the procurement of C-135s and the initiation of the C-141 development.

Since then each succeeding crisis—Berlin, Cuba and Vietnam—has underscored the importance of adequate airlift, and we have continued to expand this program. In the future, even our largest transport, the C-5A, will be able to deliver its cargo to primitive airfields well forward in the theater of operations. And where formerly only relatively light land-force equipment could be airlifted, the C-5As and C-141s will be capable of carrying virtually all types of equipment organic to Army divisions.

Besides the build-up of the airlift fleet itself, the most important measure taken to improve our rapid-response capability was the forward pre-positioning of the heavy equipment and bulk supplies which could be taken over quickly by combat units airlifted into the area. Land-based pre-positioning has been provided in Europe and the Far

East. However, there are practical limits to how far this should be carried. Therefore we decided to turn to a more flexible method of pre-positioning, using converted Victory ships as mobile depots carrying balanced loads of heavy equipment and supplies.

This approach led eventually to the development of an entirely new concept in sealift, a special ship—fast, highly efficient, tailored for its role—to complement strategic airlift. These vessels would be built for the strategic function only, to be positioned near trouble spots with a full load of combat and support equipment, or poised ready in a U.S. port. Their name fits their role: Fast Deployment Logistic Ship, or FDL.

After testing a wide range of combinations, we found the force that gives us the required capability at least cost: six C-5A squadrons, fourteen C-141 squadrons and thirty FDLs, pre-positioned equipment in Europe and in the Pacific, a Civil Reserve Air Fleet, and 460 commercial cargo ships. Still, other combinations are possible, of course, and the solution ultimately will be worked out between my successors and the Congress.

The list of new developments is almost endless, in a decade which saw technology accelerating constantly. For the layman without technical training, it is a bewildering array. There is always the danger that we are simply handing him incomprehensible terms when we tell him that the number of guided-missile surface ships has been increased from 23 to 72, or that helicopter lift capability has increased by 300 percent. Unfortunately, and for obvious reasons, we cannot be more explicit on nuclear capability, to cite one example, than to say that we have increased the number of nuclear weapons in NATO Europe by 100 percent.

Yet I would suggest that the government ought to try harder to communicate in this area. It may be too much to expect the layman to react knowledgeably to news that the Poseidon has five to ten times the destructive power of the Polaris missile. He may not grasp completely the explanation that a new rocket can carry several nuclear warheads, each proceeding independently to its target as it re-enters the atmosphere. But he ought to understand subjectively that decisions on the deployment of these weapons might be a critical piece in a broader mosaic which will determine the survival of man.

We in government have the obligation to explain our decisions to the extent security will permit; after all, it is we who should stand humbly with the power and responsibility placed in our hands, for we know the consequences if we fail.

CHAPTER SIX

✳

Managing for Defense

THE challenge of the Department of Defense is compelling. It is the greatest single management complex in history; it supervises the greatest aggregation of raw power ever assembled by man. Yet my instructions from both President Kennedy and President Johnson were simple: to determine and provide what we needed to safeguard our security without arbitrary budget limits, but to do so as economically as possible.

In many respects the role of a public manager is similar to that of a private manager. In each case he may follow one of two alternative courses. He can act either as a judge or as a leader. As the former he waits until subordinates bring him problems for solution, or alternatives for choice. In the latter case, he immerses himself in his operation, leads and stimulates an examination of the objectives, the problems and the alternatives. In my own case, and specifically with regard to the Department of Defense, the responsible choice seemed clear.

From the beginning in January, 1961, it seemed to me that the principal problem in efficient management of the Department's resources was not the lack of management authority. The National Security Act provides the Secretary of Defense a full measure of power. The problem was rather the absence of the essential management tools needed to make sound decisions on the really crucial issues of national security.

Two points seem to me axiomatic. The first is that the United States is well able to spend whatever it needs to spend on national security. The second point is that this ability does not excuse us from applying strict standards of effectiveness and efficiency to the way we spend our Defense dollars.

Within that framework, our early studies led us into three major efforts: improvement of our strategic retaliatory forces, increased emphasis on our non-nuclear forces, and a general upgrading of effectiveness and efficiency in the Defense Establishment. For that matter, the first two of our major objectives commanded wide support by the time I took office, as I mentioned earlier.

The third caused considerable controversy. Not that

there was much disagreement about the need; for years everyone who thought seriously about the Department of Defense felt that major improvements were needed. The solutions offered ranged from drastic proposals for complete unification of the armed forces to vague suggestions about "cutting the fat out of the military budget." But there was no consensus on just what should be done.

Moreover, there was an additional and inevitable human problem. These reforms would necessarily change traditional ways of doing things, and limit the customary ways of spending Defense money. It is inevitable that people will take more easily to suggestions that they should have more money to spend, as in the improvement of our nuclear and non-nuclear capabilities, than to suggestions that they must spend less or that they must abandon established ways of doing things. Yet the very substantial increases in the budget which we felt necessary added a further strong incentive, if any were needed, to move ahead on these problems of increasing efficiency and effectiveness.

What we set out to do can be divided into two parts: the first essentially a series of management reforms of the kind to be found in any well-run organization, an effort which is in large part covered by the formal Five-Year Cost Reduction Program we set up in July, 1962. The common characteristic of such reforms is that they have very little to do with military effectiveness, one way or the other. They merely save money by introducing more efficient methods of doing things.

The second and more important part of the effort did

bear directly on military effectiveness. Although dollar savings are sometimes an important by-product, here the essential point was to increase military effectiveness. We found that the three military departments had been establishing their requirements independently of each other. The results could be described fairly as chaotic: Army planning, for example, was based primarily on a long war of attrition; Air Force planning was based, largely, on a short war of nuclear bombardment. Consequently the Army was stating a requirement for stocking months, if not years, of combat supplies against the event of a sizable conventional conflict. The Air Force stock requirements for such a war had to be measured in days, and not very many days at that. Either approach, consistently followed, might make some sense. The two combined could not possibly make sense. What we needed was a coordinated strategy seeking objectives actually attainable with the military resources available. The fact was that, in the past, so-called requirements bore almost no relation to the real world: enormous requirements existed on paper, often almost entirely disembodied from the actual size and nature of the procurement program.

Our new form of budget for the first time grouped together for planning purposes units which must fight together in the event of war. The Navy strategic forces, the Polaris submarines, are now considered together with the Air Force Strategic Air Command; Navy general-purpose forces are considered together with the Army and Marine divisions and the Air Force Tactical Air Command. This kind of reform provides substantial improvement in the effectiveness of our military establishment. Even where it does not lead directly to lower expenditures, it is economical in the true sense of the word; that is, it gives us the maximum national security obtainable from the dollars we do spend. We can imagine many different kinds of wars the United States must be prepared to fight, but a war in which the Army fights independently of the Navy, or the Navy independently of the Air Force, is not one of them. Quite obviously, the coordination of the planning of the four services makes eminently good sense on the narrowest military grounds.

The situation becomes more complicated when decisions must be made on requested force-level increases or the development or procurement of new weapons. Adding a weapon to our inventory is not necessarily synonymous with adding to our national security. Moreover, even if we were to draft every scientist and engineer in the country into weapons-development work, we could still develop only a fraction of the systems that are proposed. This process of choice must begin with solid indications that a proposed system would really add something to our national security. The United States cannot even seriously consider going ahead with a full-scale weapons-system development until that basic requirement has been met.

Development costs alone on typical major weapons systems today are enormous. Over a billion dollars were spent on the atomic airplane, which was little closer to being a useful weapon when we canceled it, shortly after I took office, than it had been half a dozen years earlier.

The B-70 bomber also was an example of a weapon

which, it seemed to me, failed to meet the basic requirement for a major systems development. It happened to be a particularly expensive weapon, since to develop, procure and operate a modest force of these planes would have cost us at least $10 billion. Yet considering the weapons we already would have by the time the B-70 could be operational, it was very hard to see how this weapon would add to our national security.

In fact, the whole debate on the B-70 tended toward terms which had very little to do with the facts of the situation. There was a lot of talk about missiles versus bombers. I have no feeling about missiles versus bombers as such. If bombers serve our national interest, then we should be interested in bombers; if missiles, then we should be interested in missiles; if a mix, then we should be interested in the mix. But the B-70 would have carried no bombs. It would have attacked its target with a very complex air-launched missile system from distances of hundreds of miles. The question was not bombs versus missiles. We were all agreed that it must be missiles. The debate was about alternative launching platforms and alternative missile systems. And the particular launching platform and missile system proposed in the B-70 program just was not an effective means to accomplish the missions proposed for it. Despite the enormous controversy and criticism when development was canceled, I think there now is general agreement that the decision was sound.

Obviously one reason for restraint in choosing new

weapons systems is their growing complexity. We need to keep the number of new systems as low as possible consistent with security, in the interest of maximum reliability. The efficiency demonstrated by a weapon on a test range may drop sharply under the chaotic conditions of combat. We must avoid putting ourselves in the position of the camera bug who weighs himself down with so much specialized equipment that he actually gets poorer results than a more lightly equipped competitor. And let me add that not only do the proliferation and complication of weapons reduce dependability, but they are major factors contributing to enormous excess inventories of parts and equipment.

What becomes clear, then, is that the question of how to spend Defense dollars and how much to spend is more complicated than is often assumed. A new weapon cannot be viewed in isolation. Anyone who has been exposed to so-called brochuremanship knows that even the most outlandish notions can be dressed up to look superficially attractive. Instead, each new weapon must be considered against a wide range of issues: its place in the complex of missions to be performed; its effects on the stability of the military situation in the world; other alternatives available.

These decisions must be made ultimately with a high degree of judgment, but there is an important difference between the way we went about them and the way they used to be made. Formerly an arbitrary budget ceiling was fixed for national defense and funds were then apportioned among the services. Today we examine all our military needs, in the context of our national security in the broadest sense, and fill them accordingly.

Up to this point I have emphasized the general considerations we applied in the Defense Department after January, 1961; the goals we sought and how we set about making the decisions to reach them. As I mentioned earlier, there was no lack of management authority, but we felt sharply the need for more efficient machinery with which to exercise it.

The problem may be considered this way: in order to make crucial decisions on force levels and weapons, the President, the Secretary of Defense and Congress must have complete information focused on those questions and their place in the over-all military system. They need to know, for example, the military effectiveness and the cost of a B-52 squadron as it relates to a Minuteman missile squadron and a Polaris submarine. The data must include not only the cost of equipping these units but also the cost of manning and operating them for various periods. Only under these circumstances can the alternatives be made fully clear.

One of the first things we did in 1961 was to design a new mechanism which would provide this information and integrate it into a single, coherent management system. The product of this effort was the Planning-Programing-Budgeting System, which is now being widely applied throughout the U.S. Government and which is being introduced in foreign governments as well.

For the Defense Department, this system serves several very important purposes:

1. It provides the mechanism through which financial budgets, weapons programs, force requirements, military strategy and foreign policy objectives are all brought into balance with one another.
2. It produces the annual Five-Year Defense Program, which is perhaps the most important single management tool for the Secretary of Defense and the basis for the annual proposal to Congress.
3. It permits the top management of the Defense Department, the President and the Congress to focus their attention on the tasks and missions related to our national objectives, rather than on the tasks and missions of a particular service.
4. It provides for the entire Defense Establishment a single approved plan, projected far enough into the future to ensure that all the programs are both physically and financially feasible.

In short, the new planning system allowed us to achieve a true unification of effort within the Department without having to undergo a drastic upheaval of the entire organizational structure. It would be a shell without substance, however, were it not backed by the full range of analytic support which operations research and other modern management techniques can bring to bear on national security problems. To this end we developed highly capable systems-analysis staffs within the Office of the Secretary of Defense, the Joint Chiefs of Staff organizations and the military departments. These staffs provided the civilian and military decision-makers of the Department with an order of analytical support far higher than had ever been the case in the past. I am convinced that this approach not only leads to far sounder and more objective decisions over the long run but yields as well the maximum amount of effective defense we can buy with each Defense dollar expended.

The creation of the Defense Department stemmed directly from one of the great lessons learned in World War II: that separate land, sea and air operations were gone forever, and that in future wars the combat forces would have to be employed as teams under unified strategic direction. The National Security Act of 1947 and its subsequent amendments established the Department and shaped its basic mode of operation. Three separate military departments reporting to the Secretary of Defense were retained to train, supply, administer and support the respective land, sea and air forces. However, operational direction of the combat forces in the field was made the responsibility of the unified and specified commanders, reporting to the Secretary through the Joint Chiefs of Staff. Thus, from a functional viewpoint, the Department of Defense has been given a bilineal organizational structure. The operational control and direction of the combat forces extend down through one chain of command, and the direction and control of the supporting activities down through another. While this basic structure proved to be entirely sound and workable, we have found it necessary over the past seven years to make a number of changes in both parts of the organization.

With respect to the first chain of command, it seemed to me that two major deficiencies still remained to be corrected. Some of the combat-ready forces had not yet been placed under the unified and specified command structure. Also, the Joint Chiefs of Staff had not yet been provided the organizational and management tools they needed in order to give the most effective day-to-day operational direction to the combat forces.

To correct the first deficiency, we created in 1961 the U.S. Strike Command, putting under a single joint command the combat-ready forces of the Tactical Air Command and the Strategic Army Corps. They previously had been controlled directly by their respective military departments. With that organizational change, all combat-ready forces are now assigned within the unified and specified command structure. The Strike Command provided us with an integrated, mobile, highly combat-ready force, available to augment the unified commands overseas or to be employed as the primary force in remote areas. Moreover, as a result of the improved operational concepts developed under Strike Command and the joint training received, the entire Army–Air Force team is now better integrated and works together more efficiently and effectively than at any other time in our history.

To meet the need for better managerial tools, we carefully reviewed both the internal organization of the Joint Chiefs of Staff and the various support functions. We found that two of the most important services to field commanders—communications and intelligence—were being performed separately by the three military departments with virtually no regard for the role of the JCS in the operational direction of combat forces in the field. It was clear that both of these functions should be brought under the direct supervision of the JCS. But they were too large and diverse to be placed within the Organization of the Joint Chiefs of Staff and too important to be fragmented among the individual unified and specified commands. Accordingly, we decided to consolidate them in two new Defense agencies which report to the Secretary of Defense directly through the Joint Chiefs.

Actions were already under way in 1961 to form the Defense Communications Agency. We expanded its functions to include not only the long-haul communications facilities of the Defense Establishment, but also those required for command and control functions, intelligence, weather services, logistics and administration for all components of the Department. The intelligence functions formerly performed by the three services moved under the new Defense Intelligence Agency.

Several measures were taken to improve the organization surrounding the Joint Chiefs of Staff. A new National Military Command System was created to ensure that the JCS can continue to direct the armed forces under all foreseeable circumstances. Several new offices were added, including special assistants in such diverse areas as strategic mobility and counterinsurgency.

When we looked into the support functions, we found that organization had lagged far behind technological advance. The logistics structures of the military departments simply had not kept pace with the demands of rapidly changing technology. The inefficiencies drew repeated attention and criticism from the Congress, which continually prodded the Department in the direction of a fully unified logistics management. The Defense Establishment, however, had moved very haltingly toward that objective with various improvisations. Our solution was to create in 1961 the Defense Supply Agency. We consolidated into it the eight existing separate managers for common supplies, the manager for traffic management, the Armed Forces Supply Support Center and the surplus property sales offices. Later we assigned additional responsibilities to DSA, including the management of common electrical and electronics items, chemical supplies and industrial production equipment. All this resulted in substantial reductions in inventories and operating costs, plus wide improvements in supply services.

Before we organized the Defense Supply Agency, the various elements of the Department—to cite a typical example—were using slightly different forms for requisitions, no less than sixteen in all. As a result, nearly every time a piece of property was transferred from one part of the Department to another, a new requisition form had to be typed. By the simple expedient of establishing a common requisition form and system, we eliminated literally tens of thousands of man-hours of labor formerly wasted in having clerks retype the forms. Other minor but colorful instances of improvement were the consolidation of eighteen different types and sizes of butcher smocks, four kinds of belt buckles and six kinds of women's exercise bloomers.

In addition to these changes in the support field, many more were found necessary in the three military departments, particularly in the broad area of logistics management. In the Army the logistics functions of the old "technical services" were merged into a new Army Matériel Command. In the Navy the logistics functions performed by its bureaus were replaced by a Naval Matériel Command. In the Air Force a realignment between the Research and Development Command and the Air Matériel Command resulted in two new commands: the Air Force Systems Command and the Air Force Logistics Command. We made each of these organizational changes to meet the need for increased efficiency in the procurement and support of new weapons systems, as well as to keep pace with rapidly changing technology.

All these organizational changes were important in the improvement of Defense Department management. But in the end, economy and efficiency in the day-to-day execution of the Defense program rests largely in the hands of tens of thousands of military and civilian managers in the field. How to motivate them to do their job more efficiently, and how to determine whether or not they do so, have always been among the most difficult and elusive problems facing the top management of the Defense Department. Even where poor performance is found, the practical remedies are more limited than one would imagine. The competition for competent management personnel is extremely keen. We had no absolute assurance that the people we could hire would be any better than those we might fire. My task was to devise a management system through which I could mobilize the capabilities of the managers at the lower levels, involve them more intimately in the entire management process, and motivate them to seek out and develop more efficient ways of doing their jobs. And that in essence is the purpose of the Defense Department's Cost Reduction Program.

Since almost three-quarters of the total Defense budget is spent for logistics in the broadest sense of that term, we concentrated our efforts first on that entire process. From various studies, we were able to identify the key areas in which improvements were urgently needed and where the potential for significant savings was the greatest.

The problem was how to organize the effort on a broad continuing basis. We knew that "one-shot" efforts soon played out, leaving behind no real long-term benefits. Finally, we realized that unless the top management itself placed a high priority on the effort, managers at lower levels would soon lose interest in the program.

Initially we laid out a five-year program. Some twenty-eight distinct areas of logistics management were carefully delineated and grouped under the three major over-all objectives of the program: to buy only what we needed, to buy at the lowest sound price, and to reduce operating costs. We fixed specific annual cost-reduction goals, and designed a quarterly reporting system to measure progress against these goals. Each service Secretary and agency head

was directed to review personally the progress achieved
and to report the results to my office. I then carefully reviewed these results myself, and reported on them to the
President and the Congress each year.

We consistently tried to apply one basic test: that a re-
portable savings must result from a clearly identifiable, new
or improved management action which actually reduced
costs while fully satisfying the military requirement. I believe that by and large the savings we reported over the
years have met that basic test.

Beyond those savings—more than $14 billion during the
five-year period—the program has raised significantly the
effectiveness of our world-wide logistics system. We have
developed new procurement techniques to broaden competition for Defense work and reduce the use of cost-plus-
fixed-fee contracts. More realistic standards determine
requirements. New procedures ensure maximum use of excess inventories throughout the Department. Special staffs
were organized to eliminate unneeded frills from specifi-
cations.

With the completion of the five-year program in fiscal
1966, I established the program on an annual basis the
following year. We set a goal of $1.5 billion in savings to be
realized in three years from decisions to be made in fiscal
year 1967. The results have already exceeded our objectives. The current estimate for the three-year period
stands now at $2.059 billion.

The management task is never finished, of course, and
this is particularly true of cost reduction. Even while old

deficiencies are being corrected, entirely new ones appear. The very large savings achieved during the first five years are not likely to be duplicated during the succeeding five years, but there are a number of logistics areas where the opportunities for improvement are virtually unlimited. One in which activity will no doubt continue is the program through which we closed installations we no longer needed. In many cases they simply were surplus; in others consolidation was dictated by sound management. Altogether, we took 967 actions in the seven years, releasing 1,818,000 acres (over 3,000 square miles) of real estate and eliminating 207,047 jobs.

We recognized, of course, that this program could have serious impact on local communities and on our own employees. From the beginning, the Department worked closely with the communities affected, seeking to find other uses for the facilities we no longer needed. We guaranteed every displaced employee an offer of a new job, and guaranteed as well his former salary level for two years when he took a lower-paying job.

These, then, are the sorts of problems, large and relatively small, which fall to the Secretary of Defense. Sharp differences arise as to how much we should spend on defense and where we should spend our marginal Defense dollars. And here is where the responsibility most clearly falls upon the Secretary. At the end, these problems come down always to the same question: what is really in our national interest? Every hour of every day the Secretary is confronted by a conflict between the national interest and the parochial interests of particular industries, individual services or local areas. He cannot avoid controversy in the whole range of issues which dominate the headlines if he is to place the interest of the many above the interest of the few. And yet it is the national interest, above all, which he has sworn to serve.

PART III

✧

Where Security Lies

CHAPTER SEVEN

✦

On Gaps and Bridges

Man is the only creative animal on earth, though paradoxically his resistance to change sometimes can be almost heroically obstinate. He builds institutions in order to preserve past innovations, but in that very act often fails to promote the environment for the growth of new ones. And so there have developed the so-called gaps that trouble our times. There are several, but two of which we have heard recently, and which I want to discuss in this chapter, are the gap between the industrial nations of Western Europe and ourselves—the technological gap—and the gap that divides the young, protesting members of our society from their elders—the generation gap.

The Europeans speak of a technological gap, complaining that we are so surpassing them in industrial development that we eventually will create a kind of technological colonialism. Prime Minister Harold Wilson of Great Britain not long ago used some rather pointed language at a meeting of the Council of Europe at Strasbourg. He warned of "an industrial helotry under which we in Europe produce only the conventional apparatus of a modern economy, while becoming increasingly dependent on American business for the sophisticated apparatus which will call the industrial tune in the seventies and eighties."

The whole question got onto the agenda of NATO's ministerial meeting in Paris in 1966. The Organization for Economic Cooperation and Development published a report on the subject, and the Common Market has been deeply concerned.

Part of the problem is the so-called brain drain. Increasing numbers of foreign-born scientists and technicians are leaving the Old World for the New, not merely because of high salaries but because of the challenging and adventurous jobs available in the United States.

Without discounting the more serious implications of this matter, we ought not to become too narrowly nationalistic about it either. Brains, on the whole, are like hearts, and they go where they are appreciated. Nationalism, generally speaking, has never made much headway against love. One may doubt that nationalism by itself is going to be much more successful with the brain than it has been with the heart.

However, I do have a suggestion for Europe about the so-called brain drain. In my view, the technological gap was misnamed. It is not so much a technological gap as it is a managerial gap, and the brain drain occurs not merely because we have more advanced technology here in the United States, but rather because we have more modern and effective management.

God—the Communist commentators to the contrary—is clearly democratic. He distributes brain power universally, but He quite justifiably expects us to do something efficient and constructive with that priceless gift. That is what management is all about. Its medium is human capacity, and its most fundamental task is to deal with change. It is the gate through which social, political, economic, technological change, indeed change in every dimension, is rationally spread through society.

Some critics today worry that our democratic, free societies are becoming overmanaged. I would argue that the opposite is true. As paradoxical as it may sound, the real threat to democracy comes not from overmanagement, but from undermanagement. To undermanage reality is not to keep it free. It is simply to let some force other than reason shape reality. That force may be unbridled emotion; it may be greed; it may be aggressiveness; it may be hatred; it may be ignorance; it may be inertia; it may be anything other than reason. But whatever it is, if it is not reason that rules man, then man falls short of his potential.

Vital decision-making, particularly in policy matters,

must remain at the top. This is partly, though not completely, what the top is for. But rational decision-making depends on having a full range of rational options from which to choose, and successful management organizes the enterprise so that process can best take place. It is a mechanism whereby free men can most efficiently exercise their reason, initiative, creativity and personal responsibility. The adventurous and immensely satisfying task of an efficient organization is to formulate and analyze these options.

It is true enough that not every conceivable complex human situation can be fully reduced to lines on a graph, or to percentage points on a chart, or to figures on a balance sheet. But all reality can be reasoned about, and not to quantify what can be quantified is only to be content with something less than the full range of reason.

Modern creative management of huge, complex phenomena is impossible without both the technical equipment and technical skills which the advance of human knowledge has brought us. In my view, the industrial gap that is beginning to widen between Europe and the United States is due in large part to what we have been discussing here.

Now, how can that gap be closed? Can it be closed by boycotting American technology with high tariffs, or by prohibiting American investment in foreign countries? Can it be overcome by narrowly restricting scientific immigration? I doubt it. Can it be closed by individual countries in Europe establishing an immensely expensive and narrowly nationalistic defense industry, on the dubious economic theory that only through massive military research and development can a nation industrialize with maximum speed and benefit to its domestic economy? The answer is demonstrably no, and the proof is clear. The two overseas nations which have industrialized the most rapidly and successfully since the end of World War II are West Germany and Japan. Neither of these nations has established a domestic defense industry. How, then, can the technological gap be closed? Ultimately it can be closed only at its origin: education.

Europe is weak educationally, and that weakness is seriously crippling its growth. It is weak in its general education; it is weak in its technical education; and it is particularly weak in its managerial education. The relevant statistics are revealing. In the United Kingdom, France, Germany and Italy, for example, about 90 percent of the thirteen- and fourteen-year-old students are enrolled in school. But after age fifteen there is an abrupt and sharp drop. Fewer than 20 percent remain in school. In the United States 99 percent of the thirteen- and fourteen-year-olds are in school; but more important, even at age eighteen we still have more than 45 percent pursuing their education.

In the United Kingdom some 336,000 students are enrolled at the university level. Thus only about 10 percent of college-age individuals are attending institutions of higher learning. In Germany there are about 270,000 students at the university level, and this represents only about 7 percent of all the college-age youth. In Italy there are about 240,000 students at the university level, which, again, is only about 7 percent of the college-age group.

In France the picture is somewhat brighter. Some 400,000 students, about 15 percent of the college-age group, are receiving higher education. But compare these figures of industrialized Europe with the United States. Here we have more than four million students in college, and this represents some 40 percent of our college-age population. What is also to the point is that modern managerial education—the level of competence, say, of the Harvard Business School—is practically unknown in industrialized Europe. I cite these statistics, not to boast of American education, which, all too clearly, has its own deficiencies, but to point out that technological advance, and its two bedrock prerequisites, broad general knowledge and modern managerial competence, cannot come into being without improving the foundation of it all.

That foundation is education, right across the board. If Europe really wants to close the technological gap, it has to improve its education, both general and special, and both quantitatively and qualitatively. There is no other way to get to the taproot of the problem. I do not want to be misunderstood in all this; science and technology, and modern management, do not sum up the entire worth of education. Developing our human capabilities to the fullest is what ultimately matters most. Call it humanism, or call it whatever one likes, but that clearly is what education finally is all about. Yet without modern science and technology, and the generalist and managerial structure to go with it, progress of any kind, spiritual, humanistic, economic or otherwise, will become increasingly less possible everywhere in the world. Without this kind of progress the world is going to remain explosively backward and provincial.

The second gap, between our protesting young and their somewhat bewildered elders, is related. The times in which we live have been called the Age of Protest, and judging from the number of pickets on our nation's sidewalks, it does not seem an altogether unappropriate title. If one reads the many millions of words written on the subject, it is not entirely clear who is doing the more protesting: the young people against their elders or the elders against their children. There are grounds for believing that the 1960s are not the first time the older generation has protested against the young. But what about the protests of the younger generation, and especially the college generation?

For those worried parents who believe that campus problems began with Berkeley in 1964, it may be instructive to read of the riots at the University of Paris in 1228 and at Oxford in 1355. It is true that they were not so much sit-ins as they were drink-ins since the trouble usually began in a tavern, but they did involve the relationship of civil authority and the university's autonomy, and they make events at Berkeley not long ago look tame by comparison.

As a matter of fact, a survey of more than seven hundred college presidents on the subject of student protests revealed that, contrary to popular belief, most student demonstrations today do not involve the war in Vietnam, or civil rights, or political issues at all. Most of the protests, it seems, are about allowing students more say in university administration, educational policy or various housing regulations.

Even so, there is a serious, even grave, dimension to the protest among many students today. But whatever comfort some of the extremist protest may be giving our enemies, and it is clear that this is the case, let us be clear about our principles and our priorities. This is a nation in which the freedom of dissent is fundamental, and beneath its specific protests there runs a generalized theme in most of the serious student discussion. It is the fear that somehow society, all society—East and West—has fallen victim to a bureaucratic tyranny of technology that is gradually depersonalizing and alienating modern man himself.

In its roots this may be a nameless fear, but it is clearly not altogether a new one. Man has always trembled a bit before his tools, and there always has been an intrinsic ambivalence in technology. The cave man, for example, discovered that a stone ax was a decided improvement over a pointed stick in dispatching the wild animals in the neighborhood. Then he discovered to his dismay that it also was a fairly fearful instrument in the hands of a disgruntled neighbor who in a sudden burst of unneighborliness might wish to dispatch him as well. The enterprising visionary who first invented the wheel found to his delight, no doubt, that he could ride a lot more comfortably than he could run; but if he was anything like our contemporaries, he probably also discovered that the wheel could not only run faster than the pedestrian, it could also run over him.

Today our tools are more complex, but they are no less

ambivalent in their moral applicability. We can use thermo-nuclear power to dig a new Panama Canal or we can use it to dig a new mass grave for humanity. At Berkeley students carried signs reading: "I am a human being; do not fold, bend or mutilate." It is a sentiment we can all emphatically agree with; I wish very much that college students in Peking and Hanoi were allowed to carry the same signs on their campuses.

But for many students in America the computer has become the primordial symbol of mass impersonalization. It is ironical that this should be so considering the immense quantum of human drudgery, both mental and manual, that the computer has eliminated. It has been the American practice from the beginning to take work loads off the backs of men and put them onto the backs of machines. We have done that not so much because we have valued machines in themselves but because we have valued man more.

The argument against modern tools like the computer is, ultimately, an argument against reason itself. Not that a computer is a substitute for reason; quite the contrary, it is a product of reason and it assists us in the application of reason. But to argue that some phenomena transcend precise measurement—which is true enough—is no excuse for neglecting the arduous task of carefully analyzing what *can* be measured. A computer does not substitute for judgment any more than a pencil substitutes for literacy. But writing ability without a pencil is no particular advantage.

In any event, it seems a little premature to worry about a computer being on the verge of replacing the human brain.

Quite apart from anything else, that brain is an utterly incredible computer itself, probably the most magnificent bit of miniaturization in the universe. Though it weighs only about three pounds, it contains some ten billion nerve cells, each of which has some 25,000 possible interconnections with other nerve cells. It has been calculated that to build an electronic computer large enough to have that range of choice would require an area equal to the entire surface of the earth. As St. Augustine observed, man looks about the universe in awe at its wonders and forgets that he himself is the greatest wonder of all.

But it is also true that the ambivalence of technology grows with its own complexity, and *Homo faber*, Man the Maker, is wise continually to question whether it is he or his tools who are in charge. As yet there is no definitive answer to the question, but there is a definitive need to keep asking it. Clearly the real question is not whether we should have tools but only whether we are becoming tools. It is not really the computer that is in question; it is whether or not Dr. Strangelove is sitting at the console.

It is too simple an answer to reply that technology itself is morally neutral and that man must simply take care to retain his human control. The more profound question is whether or not complex technology narrows or widens the alternatives available for human control. It is clear enough that man conditions his technology; what is less clear is the extent to which technology conditions man. The degree and moral quality of that conditioning is a dilemma we must face, but we must face it and solve it and not merely fall into an escapist and emotional romanticism.

One of the most refreshing qualities of the campus ferment is its intense inner-directedness and its frankly philosophical bent. One student observed: "We don't automatically accept the value of institutions." Another added flatly: "Our quarrel is with Aristotle; we say man is *not* a social animal."

As much as one might be tempted to disagree with those sentiments, it is marvelous to hear university students seriously quarreling with Aristotle again. It may even symbolize the renaissance of metaphysics from the swampland of semanticism where it has been bogged down for so long.

It is understandable that the tendency of contemporary man standing in awe of his own technology should be to look back to a simpler and more secure pattern of society in which the individual could assert more fully his own independence. That is a strong tendency in our own Jeffersonian tradition which quite rightly puts such decisive emphasis on man's independence. The irony, of course, is that Jefferson was himself a brilliant technological innovator, as anyone who has explored Monticello would agree, and it is unlikely that today Jefferson would fret much about being folded, bent or mutilated by the computer. It is somewhat more likely that he would invent a better one.

The fact is that an honest inspection of history reveals not so much a nostalgic series of Golden Ages in which men led the Good Life as, on the contrary, a rather dismal series of golden opportunities that men foolishly passed up which might have accomplished precisely that. All of this is intimately related to man's education, but is modern education really relevant to the human condition?

No age in history has ever had a thornier bout with relevancy than ours, and the reason seems clear. We are caught up in a new dimension of explosive change that has no precedent in the one million years of man's experience. If we had been educated in third-century B.C. Athens, or in fourth-century Byzantium or fourteenth-century Bologna, we might reasonably have assumed that the education we received as a child would still be meaningful in our old age. Change took place, of course, even in the ancient and medieval worlds, but the rate of change relative to a man's life span was slow enough to guarantee that the quantum of knowledge acquired in youth would remain valid into old age.

What has happened today is that the progression of technological and social change is no longer merely arithmetical —it is geometric. An engineer, for example, will find that ten years from his graduation fully half his expensively acquired engineering education is already obsolete, and that the other 50 percent of knowledge he will then require to stay relevant has not even been discovered. This galloping ratio of radical change is a problem not only for the engineer. It is a problem for anyone: the poet, the philosopher, the teacher—for anyone who wishes to remain relevant in his own society.

None of us fully understands the inner dynamics of this calculus of relevancy. More often than not we are content simply to state the problem rather than to think hard about the answers. It is easy enough to wring one's hands over the complicated issues of meaning and value that a time of radical change implies. It is much tougher to tackle these issues honestly and humbly and work toward wise solutions.

Sometimes we do not even state the problem in a wholly realistic way. We fear that organization in modern society is growing too big and too complex and that we are establishing management controls that are too massive. We describe complex organization as a depersonalized bureaucracy and brand it an Orwellian nightmare. But it is possible that exactly the reverse is the case, that some of our gravest problems in society arise not from overmanagement but out of undermanagement, that democracy can become non-participating precisely to the degree that organic and hierarchical management breaks down.

Exploding urbanization, to take a serious example, has been a fact of life in the Western world for more than two hundred years; it has brought in its wake massive social turbulence and tension. Now it is sweeping the developed world like a blight, but there is no evidence that man has overmanaged this problem; there is much evidence that he has undermanaged it.

As all forms of social, economic, political and even religious organization grow larger and more complex, we might do well to ponder the fate of the Brontosaurus, the most magnificent of all the dinosaurs. He grew to be eighty feet long and was the most massive anatomical specimen of antiquity. He was a case, however, of classic undermanagement, for though he weighed an incredible forty tons, he had only a golf-ball-sized brain of some three ounces. He could not accommodate to change, could not remain relevant to his environment, and magnificent as he was he disappeared.

The observable fact is that most forms of social organization are growing more complex. But complexity itself is not necessarily inferior to simplicity, and simple arrangements, by the mere fact of their simplicity, are not invariably more democratic. In the Judeo-Christian dispensation the first human organization was a very simple one, one man and one woman, one Adam and one Eve. The organization was simple, but they managed to get one another into an extraordinary amount of difficulty. Even the first fraternal organization we read about was ideally simple. There were two brothers, one Cain and one Abel; the arrangement was very unbureaucratic, but the outcome was classically undemocratic.

All of this is immensely relevant to that generalized uneasiness that we are all being drawn into a Kafkaesque world in which science and technology encroach dangerously on the realm of the spirit. If there is a danger of depersonalization in our society, then it is our rationally protesting young who are well endowed to save us from that threat. It is their special gift, and it is the world's special need.

Robert Frost, in one of his most pensive moods, wrote:

> Two roads diverged in a wood, and I—
> I took the one less traveled by,
> And that has made all the difference.

The education of the young is unfortunately never a detailed road map. It is a passport into a dense wood, filled with forked roads. For our protesting younger generation, many of those roads will be the ones less traveled by. But if they choose wisely, it can be a rewarding journey. Indeed, it will be much more than a journey; it will be a discovery. What they will discover is not that there is an unbridgeable gap between the generations, but rather those truths which we all, young and old alike, seek to know: who we are and Whose wood this is in which we walk.

✦

CHAPTER EIGHT

New Missions

DESPITE its awesome power and the world-wide sweep of its activities, the basic mission of the Department of Defense is simply stated. That mission is military security; or, more broadly, to maintain in constant readiness the military forces necessary to protect the nation from attack, keep its commitments abroad and support its foreign policy.

Beyond that central mission of combat readiness, however, security is a broad concept. During my seven years in the Department it seemed to me that those vast resources could contribute to the attack on our tormenting social problems, both supporting our basic mission and adding to the quality of our national life. For, in the end, poverty and social injustice may endanger our national security as much as any military threat.

The Defense Department set out to make its contribution through three programs: "Open Housing," to break down racial discrimination in off-base housing for military personnel; "Project 100,000," to salvage each year 100,000 young men who were caged and oppressed by poverty, first for two years of military service and then for productive civilian lives; and "Project Transition," to prepare more of the three-quarters of a million men leaving military service annually for a positive role in society.

Open housing was a most obvious avenue for action, since racial discrimination, despite recent legislative advances, remains an infection in our national life. The Defense Department, beginning with the courageous executive order of President Truman which integrated the armed services in 1948, has been a powerful fulcrum in removing the barriers to racial justice, not merely in the military but in the country at large. But the nation's road to equality is still strewn with boulders of prejudice.

Shortly after I became Secretary of Defense, I asked Gerhard A. Gesell, a leading attorney, to direct a review of progress toward equal opportunity in the armed forces. His committee took a hard, realistic look at the problem. It reported that substantial improvement had been made on military bases, but it found that severe off-base discrimination affected thousands of Negro servicemen and their families. This discrimination was most destructive in the field of housing.

Open housing is a serious issue throughout our society. But this intolerable racial discrimination affects military personnel even more severely than it does the population at large. The serviceman and his family, on limited compensation and under military orders, must move every few years. While defending his nation he is singularly defenseless against this bigotry.

My response to the Gesell Committee findings was to issue a directive incorporating its recommendations. Commanders everywhere were asked to organize voluntary programs to eliminate housing discrimination in the communities surrounding their bases. In the Pentagon we turned our minds to other problems.

Early in 1967 we reviewed the results of that four-year-old directive. Teams were sent to a dozen bases to look into every aspect of equal opportunity. A special task force was set up for the greater Washington area. Seventeen thousand service families were surveyed and their answers were analyzed. One fact became painfully clear: the voluntary program had failed, and failed miserably.

This failure we found intolerable. Our nation should not and will not ask a Negro sergeant, for example, to risk his life day after dangerous day in the heat and hardship of a jungle war and then bring him home and compel him to remain separated from his wife and his children because of the hate and prejudice that parade under the pomposity of racial superiority. Yet that is precisely what has been happening in this country. The color of the blood that our men shed in the defense of Asia is all the same, but when these men return home, it is not the color of their blood that matters but the color of their skin.

Thousands of our Negro troops who have returned from Vietnam are victims of discrimination in off-base housing. When there is adequate housing on the base, Negro men in uniform are treated as all Americans should be treated. When there is not, and the Negro must depend on the civilian community for housing, he all too often is denied this equality of treatment. Because of his color he, his family and our national security suffer a penalty because of the impaired morale of our fighting forces.

This is a group of men who have distinguished themselves in the service of their nation. It is a fact that Negroes often volunteer for the most difficult and hazardous assignments. It is a fact that 20 percent of the Army men who died in Vietnam in 1967 were Negroes. The Negro serviceman has been loyal and responsible to his country, but the people of his country have failed him.

Our original voluntary program floundered and fell apart. It lacked sufficient leadership from the top, starting with me, and going right down through the senior echelon of the Defense Establishment; and it lacked appropriately stiff sanctions for violation of our antidiscrimination policy.

We forged, therefore, a whole new set of tools to deal with this failure. The first phase was to compile a nationwide census of open off-base rental housing for military personnel. The second phase was to mobilize throughout the country effective community support for nondiscriminatory military off-base housing. The greater Washington metropolitan area, including Maryland and Virginia, was chosen as our first objective. We wanted to make the area surrounding the nation's capital a model program, as it should be, and we wanted to learn quickly all the lessons we could that would assist us in the country at large.

Officials from the highest levels of the Defense Department, the Deputy Secretary of Defense, the service Secretaries, and senior commanders, met with realtors and landlords of the area and put the matter to them squarely. The extent of off-base housing discrimination was appalling. The morale of Negro servicemen and their families was being severely eroded. We told the landlords the Defense Department could no longer tolerate the situation, and we appealed to them for voluntary compliance with our nondiscriminatory housing policy. But we pointed out that the situation as it stood was so unjust that, whether or not we secured their voluntary compliance, we simply could not permit the conditions to continue. If the landlords felt they would not or could not comply, we were going to have to prohibit any of our men—regardless of their race—from signing rental agreements in housing units where such discrimination was practiced.

Many proprietors complied voluntarily, but too many did not. In many instances their position, while shortsighted, was understandable. Some faced genuine economic pressures. In any event, they did not comply, and we were compelled to take the only action open to us. We prohibited all military personnel from signing new leases or rental agreements in their facilities. This applied a countervailing economic pressure, and our open-housing program took on an altogether new and positive direction. In northern Virginia and Maryland we more than trebled the number of nondiscriminatory units, from about 15,000 to 53,000 units within 120 days.

The program is now at work elsewhere throughout the nation. There is an intensified program in California at this writing. We gave particular emphasis to this state, not merely because of the large number of Defense installations and military personnel there, but because California among the fourteen states with open-housing laws had the lowest percentage of apartments open to all races.

Everywhere our approach has been the same. We survey the local situation at each military base. We request cooperation and seek voluntary compliance. The Department will do everything possible to see that our military families act as good tenants: that they pay their obligations promptly and that they respect the property of private owners. I am fully aware that the Defense Department is not a philanthropic foundation or a social-welfare institution. But the Department does not intend to let our Negro servicemen and their families continue to suffer the injustices and indignities they have in the past. I am certain my successors will pursue the same policy.

Project 100,000, our second undertaking with social programs, grew out of the appalling draft rejection rate. In

1966 about 1.8 million young men reached military service age in the United States, but almost 600,000—fully a third—failed to qualify under our draft standards. Some had medical problems, but I was concerned particularly about those tens of thousands who failed because of educational deficiencies. In some areas the failure rate for draftees ran as high as 60 percent, and for Negroes in some states it exceeded 80 percent. What this clearly meant was that the burden of military service was not being shouldered equally. The inequities were serious: inequities by region, inequities by race and inequities by educational level. What was even worse was the obvious implication. If so massive a number of our young men were educationally unqualified for even the least complicated tasks of military service, how could they reasonably be expected to lead productive and rewarding lives in an increasingly technological and highly skilled society?

Department studies confirmed that a great number of those rejected were the hapless and hopeless victims of poverty. Serious poverty is not merely socially corrosive, but is intrinsically self-perpetuating. Poor nations, like poor individuals, cannot be helped until they begin to help themselves. But poverty is a social and political paralysis that atrophies ambition and drains away hope. It saps the strength of nations, not so much because it implies a lack of exploitable material resources, which often it does not, as because it withers and weakens the human potential necessary to develop them.

Poverty is not a simple concept, a mere absence of wealth.

It is a complex of debilitating conditions, each reinforcing the other in an ever-tightening web of human impairment. Illiteracy, disease, hunger and hopelessness are characteristics which of their own momentum spiral human aspirations downward. Poverty begets poverty, passing from generation to generation in a cruel cycle of near-inevitability. It endures until carefully designed outside assistance intervenes and radically redirects its internal dynamics.

Internal upheaval all across the southern half of the planet this past decade has been related directly to the explosive tensions that poverty spawns. The other face of this coin is that the pestilence of poverty has infected our own plentiful nation. Poverty in the United States is a social cancer; an exact metaphor, for cancer grows within a body, hidden from view, its malevolent presence often undetected. Poverty in America does not readily show its face to the world, for our society is conspicuously abundant beyond belief. So psychologically unexpected is poverty in the midst of overwhelming prosperity that it remains largely unrecognized even by many Americans. That one out of every six Americans should be locked in its grip seems nearly incredible, yet it is tragically true. These 32 million Americans live in every state, in every county and in every city of the nation. Nearly half of them are children, their lives still before them, and yet already blighted from the beginning if the poverty pattern in which they are trapped is allowed to play itself out.

Poverty abroad leads to unrest, to internal upheaval, to violence and to the escalation of extremism, and it does the same within our own borders. We think of ourselves—and rightly so—as a relatively stable and well-ordered society, as a society dedicated to the rule of law, and as a society free of the pathological need to resort to open violence in the streets. Yet since the end of World War II the governors of our states have had to call out military forces, combat-equipped National Guard troops, more than a hundred times to put down disorders that could not be controlled by the police. In most of these emergencies factors related directly to poverty were involved.

We need not look as far as Africa, or Asia, or Latin America for poverty-induced tensions that erupt into irrational violence. It has often happened right here in the United States, and it is certain to happen many times again until—and unless—the complex syndrome of poverty-in-the-midst-of-plenty is better understood and ultimately eliminated.

Poverty in America affects our national security, too, by its appalling waste of talent. In the technological revolution that is sweeping over the second half of our century the prime national resource becomes more and more the potential of the human brain. Innovation, technical breakthroughs, and research and development now affect defense capabilities more than any other factors.

Only 14 percent of the more than three million men in our armed forces fire weapons as their primary duty. A full 50 percent must be trained in technical skills. Human talent, therefore, is our nation's most essential resource. It cannot be mined from the ground, or harvested from the fields, or synthesized in a test tube. The 32 million Americans who are poor were not born without intellectual potential. They were not brain-poor at birth, but only privilege-poor, advantage-poor, opportunity-poor. To the extent that this nation loses the performance potential of these millions of human beings, this nation's ultimate security is diminished.

Within those considerations, the startling draft rejection rate represented an even more measurable and concrete example of the manner in which poverty has affected our national security. What many of these men badly needed was a sense of personal achievement, a sense of succeeding at a task, a sense of their own intrinsic potential. They had potential, but the poverty virus had paralyzed it in many of them. They grew up in an atmosphere of drift and discouragement. It was not simply the sometimes squalid ghettos of their external environment that debilitated them, but an internal and more destructive ghetto of personal disillusionment and despair: a ghetto of the spirit. Chronic failures in school throughout their childhood, they were destined to a sense of defeat and decay in a skill-oriented nation that requires from its manpower pool an increasing index of competence, discipline and self-confidence.

Many of these men, we decided, could be saved. The Department set out to give them the benefit of its experience in educational innovation and on-the-job training, in an atmosphere of high motivation and morale, and transformed them into competent military personnel. Beyond that, after their tour of duty, they could return to civilian life equipped with new skills and attitudes and thus break out of the self-perpetuating poverty cycle.

After close study, I was convinced that at least 100,000

men a year who were being rejected for military service, including tens of thousands of volunteers, could be accepted. To make this possible, I felt we needed only to use fully and imaginatively the resources at hand. The Defense Department today is the largest single educational complex in history. The services provide enlisted men with professional training in some 1,500 different skills in more than 2,000 separate courses. In addition, 65,000 officers a year continue their professional education. The Department operates 327 dependents' schools around the world, employing 6,800 classroom teachers for 166,000 students, making it the ninth largest U.S. school system, with a budget of $90 million. More than 30 correspondence-school centers are sponsored by the military departments, offering over 2,000 courses and enrolling nearly a million students scattered about the globe. The United States Armed Forces Institute currently has enrolled more than 250,000 students in hundreds of courses ranging from the elementary school level through college. During the five years through 1967, an annual average of 95,000 individuals earned a high school diploma or its equivalent through this hugely beneficial program.

This immense educational complex exists specifically for the needs of the Defense Department, but it nevertheless has a gigantic spin-off into American society as a whole. The services return over half a million personnel annually to the country's skilled manpower pool. A very substantial number of civilians currently employed in such skilled occupational fields as electronics, engineering, transportation management, machine-tool operation, automotive and aircraft maintenance, and the building trades—to mention only a few—have been trained in the armed forces.

Thus the imperatives of national security in our technological age make the Defense Department the world's largest educator of highly skilled men. Those same imperatives require that it also be the world's most efficient educator. As a result, the Defense Department has pioneered some of the most advanced teaching techniques. Indeed, it has been in the vanguard of a series of innovations in education technology. Its findings and its philosophy are making a significant contribution to the modernization that is sweeping throughout the American school system.

One of the Department's key concepts holds that traditional classroom training is often largely irrelevant to actual on-the-job performance requirements. By pruning from existing courses all nonessential information, we found that we could not only substantially shorten the training period, but, more important, we could increase dramatically the students' success at learning.

We experimented with programed instruction, carefully designed and matched specifically against on-the-job requirements, and allowing the student to proceed at his own individual pace rather than merely to be herded along at an arbitrarily determined group pace. We have broken new pedagogical ground in the Defense Department in order to accomplish this. So successful, for example, was the use of closed-circuit television in Defense training that the

Army established an entire individual-training television network. The great merit of closed-circuit TV is its flexibility. A low-aptitude student can use video tapes as an aid to his formal instruction and end by becoming as proficient as a high-aptitude student.

Indeed, the whole concept of "low-aptitude" and "high-aptitude" now needs redefinition. What do these designations really mean? One thing is certain: they mean something very different from what we have believed in the past. There is now ample evidence that many aptitude evaluations have less to do with how well the student can learn than with the cultural value system of the educator. Too many instructors look at a reticent or apathetic or even hostile student and conclude: "He is a low-aptitude learner." In most cases it would be more realistic for the instructor to take a hard honest look in the mirror and conclude: "I am a low-aptitude teacher."

Students differ greatly in their learning patterns. It is the educator's responsibility to become familiar with that pattern in each individual case and to build on it. More exactly, it is the educator's responsibility to create the most favorable conditions under which the student himself can build on his own learning pattern at his own pace. Ultimately it is not the teacher who teaches at all; it is the student who teaches himself. Aquinas in the thirteenth century and Aristotle fifteen hundred years before him both suggested that a teacher cannot, strictly speaking, be the *cause* of the student's knowledge, but only the *occasion* of it. Modern educational psychology confirms this. But instead of striving to be the inspiring occasions of their students' knowledge, too many teachers end by causing their students to retreat into a mental fog of boredom, confusion and noncomprehension. This mix of understandable reactions is then all too often simply labeled "low-aptitude."

We discovered within the Department of Defense that the prime reason many men "fail" the aptitude tests given at the time of induction is simply that these tests are geared to the psychology of traditional, formal, classroom, teacher-paced instruction. These tests inevitably reflect the cultural value systems and verbal patterns of affluent American society. That is why so many young men from poverty backgrounds do poorly in the tests. It is not because they do not possess basic and perhaps even brilliant intelligence, but because their cultural environment is so radically different from that assumed by the designers of the tests.

It is, for example, a generally accepted value of American society to want to "achieve" something in life. That is a sound value, but it is a value alien to many young people from poverty-encrusted environments. In their world, achievement is seldom advanced as a value, because it does not exist as a realistic possibility. Such a person appears to have "low aptitude" by conventional standards since he seems poorly motivated. But clearly a more accurate way to measure his "aptitude" is to place him in a situation that offers the encouragement he has never had before. That means a good teacher and a good course of instruction, well supported by self-paced, audio-visual aids. It also means less formal theoretical instruction in the classroom and more practical on-the-job training. Under these conditions the so-called "low-aptitude" student can succeed.

Our goal was to take 40,000 men in the first year; we actually took 49,000. They entered all the services: Army, Navy, Air Force and the Marine Corps. What sort of background did these men come from? About 60 percent were whites and about 40 percent Negroes. Their average age was twenty-one. Thirty percent of them were unemployed at the time they came to us, and an additional 26 percent were earning less than $60 a week.

What this means is that more than half of these men had been held in the grip of poverty. Nor is that surprising; their average reading score was on a bare sixth-grade level and 14 percent of them read at a third-grade level or less. Many were poorly motivated when they reached us; they lacked initiative, pride and ambition. If nothing were done to give them a strong sense of their own worth and potential, they, their wives and their children almost inevitably would be the unproductive recipients of some form of welfare payments ten years from now. I want to repeat: we took these men into the service because we were convinced that given the proper environment and training they could contribute just as much to the defense of their country as men from the more advantaged segments of our society.

To say that we were encouraged by the first year's results would be an understatement. Ninety-eight percent of our traditional categories of recruits successfully graduated from basic training during the year. The successful graduation rate of these 49,000 new-category men was 96 percent. I insisted that these men should never be singled out or stigmatized as a special group. Technically, and for our own internal record-keeping, men who formerly would have been rejected are now termed New Standards men. But the men themselves are never told that they are in this category; it is imperative that they believe in themselves and their own potential. They obviously cannot do that if we treat them with anything remotely suggesting condescension.

The plain fact is that Project 100,000 is succeeding beyond even the most hopeful expectations. Many of the commanders report that these men are turning out to be even more highly motivated than some servicemen with much more privileged backgrounds. These were the initial results, and are immensely encouraging. But obviously the real test is going to come later, when these men move back into civilian society. How will they fare then? Will the vital sense of achievement and self-confidence they have experienced in their military service, as well as the skills they have learned, move them forward in society; or will they return to the depressing downward-spiraling poverty phenomenon that plagues our urban ghettos and our rural pockets of economic stagnation?

Last fall we opened a careful follow-up study to test conclusively the ultimate outcome of Project 100,000. At least a decade of careful measurement of performance by men both in and out of the services will be required, but I am willing to make a prediction. I am convinced that the

Project 100,000 men will continue to do a fully creditable job in the services, and that on return to civilian life their earning capacity and their over-all achievement in society will be two or three times what they would have been had there been no such program. Hundreds of thousands of men can be salvaged from the blight of poverty, and the Defense Department, with no detriment whatever to its primary role, is particularly well equipped to salvage them. The benefit to our society and to the ultimate roots of our security will be enormous.

The third Defense Department program in this field has the same goal as the second basic purpose behind Project 100,000, that is, the preparation of men for a productive life as civilians after discharge. Many of the more than 750,000 who leave the services annually can move readily into civilian jobs, but a significant number face genuine problems. A survey showed that about 50 percent of those about to leave the service needed and wanted help in making the transition.

To provide that help we created a voluntary program, Project Transition, for men with 30 to 180 days of service time remaining. The plan gives priority to certain groups: to those disabled in battle; to those with no previous civilian occupation; to combat-arms servicemen with no civilian-related skill; to those who have such a skill but who require additional training or upgrading; and finally to those who desire a completely new civilian skill regardless of their current training status. The program meets four basic needs of the man leaving the service: counseling, skill enhancement, education and job placement.

Other federal agencies such as the Labor Department, Health, Education, and Welfare, and the Postal Service, as well as state and local agencies, agreed to help. A number of police departments around the nation, for example, are participating not only with professional advice and technical assistance but with solid job offers as well. Though the program was still in its pilot stage as this book was being prepared, it clearly has tremendous potential, and industrial leaders throughout the nation have already expressed enthusiasm for the idea. Furthermore, the Ford Foundation has offered to work closely with us in solving the problems connected with placing the right veteran in the right job. Every man who has served his country in the armed forces deserves the opportunity to move back usefully and productively into civilian life.

The point we must realize is this: there is no question but that the economic, social and educational legislation of the current period eventually will transform American society immensely for the better. But the very magnitude of the task will require a decade or two before the full effects can be felt. This means that the present generation of under-privileged youth of all races, caught in the self-perpetuating trap of poverty, are in danger of being left out of these eventual benefits. The United States cannot be satisfied with that situation; we must find ways to assist people now, even before our present legislation can reach its full potential for economic and social improvement.

This is manifestly not primarily a Department of Defense but a national responsibility. The Department's primary responsibility, to repeat, is the security of this nation. But in the last analysis the foundation of that security is a stable social structure. The Defense Department has the potential to contribute to the development of such a structure without compromising the combat readiness of its forces.

These three social programs are the kinds of programs that will bolster the security of this nation. They are the kinds of programs that will reduce the criticism that the United States is often bludgeoned with internationally, criticism—some of it justified—that grows out of the discrepancy between our traditional preaching of the principles of liberty and equality and our obvious lapses in the practice of those two bedrock constitutional guarantees. They are partial answers to the basic question: can our present American society afford to meet simultaneously its responsibilities both at home and abroad? I say again that we can. That we may choose not to attempt to is another matter entirely.

Let us not blame the lack of effort on the myth that we cannot do all that needs doing, for the fact is, we can. We can curb aggression abroad; we can meet our pressing social problems here at home; and we can do both at the same time if we will use wisely the resources we have.

CHAPTER NINE

The Essence of Security

FROM all that has been said here, some of the basic components of power remain obviously and tragically unchanged. Great military might remains indispensable. Because science has produced the new weapons of colossal destruction, the United States must maintain its nuclear arsenal; not only must it be maintained, but it must be so large as to deter any nation from forcing its use. Because there are those who still would test our will and undermine us slowly with subversion and limited wars, we must arm with conventional forces in common defense with our allies. These are the old realities, shaped to the world of today. But there are new realities as well, and we have been too slow to recognize them. For the fact remains that a negative and narrow notion of defense still clouds our vision and distorts national policy.

There is among us an almost ineradicable tendency to think of our security problem as being exclusively a military problem, and to think of the military problem as being exclusively a weapons or manpower problem. The truth is that contemporary man still conceives of war and peace in much the same stereotyped terms that his ancestors did. The fact that these ancestors, both recent and remote, were conspicuously unsuccessful at avoiding war and enlarging peace doesn't seem to reduce our capacity for clichés. We still tend to conceive of national security almost solely as a state of armed readiness, a vast, awesome arsenal of weaponry. We still tend to assume that it is primarily this purely military ingredient that creates security. We are haunted by this concept of military hardware.

How limited a concept this actually is becomes apparent when one ponders the kind of peace that exists, for example, between the United States and Canada. Here are two modern nations, highly developed technologically, each with immense territory, both enriched with great reserves of natural resources, each militarily sophisticated and yet divided by an unguarded frontier of thousands of miles. There is not the remotest set of circumstances in any imaginable time frame of the future in which these two nations would wage war on one another. It is so unthinkable an idea as to be absurd; but why is that so?

Canada and the United States are at peace for reasons that have nothing to do with mutual military readiness. We are at peace, truly at peace, because of the vast fund of compatible beliefs, common principles and shared ideals. We have our differences and our diversity, but the whole point is that our mutual basis for peace has nothing whatever to do with military hardware.

Obviously, and to repeat, this is not to say that the concept of military deterrence is no longer relevant in the contemporary world. Unhappily, it is still critically relevant with respect to our potential adversaries, but it has no relevance between the United States and Canada. We are not adversaries, we are not going to become adversaries, and it is not mutual military deterrence that keeps us from becoming adversaries. It is mutual respect for common principles. I mention this, as obvious as it is, simply as a kind of *reductio ad absurdum* of the concept that military hardware is the exclusive or even the primary ingredient of permanent peace in the mid-twentieth century.

In the United States, since 1961, we have achieved a considerably improved balance in our total military posture. That was the mandate I received from Presidents Kennedy and Johnson, and with their support and that of Congress we were able to create a strengthened force structure of land, sea and air components, with a vast increase in mobility and matériel, and with a massive superiority in nuclear retaliatory power over any combination of potential adversaries. Our capabilities for nuclear, conventional and countersubversive war have all been broadened and improved, and we accomplished this through military budgets that were, in fact, lesser percentages of our Gross National Product than in the past.

From the standpoint of combat readiness the United States has never been militarily stronger, and we intend to maintain that readiness. But if we think carefully about the matter, it is clear that this purely military posture is not the central element in our security. A nation can reach the point at which it does not buy more security for itself simply by buying more military hardware, and we are at that point. The decisive factor for a powerful nation already adequately armed is the character of its relationships that preserve its own intrinsic security.

First, we have to help protect those developing countries which genuinely need and request our help and which as an essential precondition are willing and able to help themselves. Second, we have to encourage and achieve a more effective partnership with those nations which can and should share international peace-keeping responsibilities. Third, we must do all we realistically can to reduce the risk of conflict with those who might be tempted to take up arms against us. Let us examine these three sets of relationships in detail: first, the developing nations.

Roughly one hundred countries today are caught up in the difficult transition from traditional to modern societies. There is no uniform rate of progress among them, and they range from primitive societies, fractured by tribalism and held feebly together by the slenderest of political sinews, to relatively sophisticated countries well on the road to agricultural sufficiency and industrial competence. This sweeping surge of development, particularly across the southern half of the globe, has no parallel in history. It has turned traditionally listless areas of the world into seething caldrons of change. On the whole it has not been a very peaceful process.

In the eight years through late 1966 alone there were no less than 164 internationally significant outbreaks of violence, each of them specifically designed as a serious challenge to the authority or the very existence of the government in question. Eight-two different governments were directly involved, and what is striking is that only 15 of these 164 significant resorts to violence were military conflicts between two states, and not a single one of the 164 conflicts was a formally declared war. Indeed, there has not been a formal declaration of war anywhere in the world since World War II.

The planet is becoming a more dangerous place to live on not merely because of a potential nuclear holocaust but also because of the large number of *de facto* conflicts and because the trend of such conflicts is growing rather than diminishing. At the beginning of 1958 there were 23 prolonged insurgencies going on around the world. As of February, 1966, there were 40. Further, the total number of outbreaks of violence has increased each year: in 1958 there were 34; in 1965 there were 58.

What is most significant of all is that there is a direct and constant relationship between the incidence of violence and the economic status of the countries afflicted. The

World Bank divides nations on the basis of per capita income into four categories: rich, middle-income, poor and very poor. The rich nations are those with a per capita income of $750 or more per year. The current U.S. level is more than $2,900, and there are 27 of these rich nations. They possess 75 percent of the world's wealth, though roughly only 25 percent of the world's population. Since 1958 only one of these 27 nations has suffered a major internal upheaval on its own territory.

But observe what happens at the other end of the economic scale. Among the 38 very poor nations, those with a per capita income of under $100 a year, no less than 32 have suffered significant conflicts. Indeed, they suffered an average of two major outbreaks of violence per country in the eight-year period. That is a great deal of conflict, and, what is worse, it has been predominantly conflict of a prolonged nature.

The trend holds predictably constant in the case of two other categories, the poor and middle-income nations. Since 1958, 87 percent of the very poor nations, 69 percent of the poor nations and 48 percent of the middle-income nations suffered serious violence. There can be no question but that there is a relationship between violence and economic backwardness, and the trend of such violence is up, not down.

Perhaps it would be somewhat reassuring if the gap between the rich nations and the poor nations were closing and if economic backwardness were significantly receding. But it is not; the economic gap is widening. By 1970 over one-half of the world's population will live in the independent nations which encircle the southern half of the planet. But this hungering half of the human race will by then command only one-sixth of the world's total of goods and services. By 1975 the dependent children of these nations alone, children under fifteen years of age, will equal the total population of the developed nations to the north.

Even in our own abundant societies we have reason enough to worry over the tensions that coil and tighten among underprivileged young people and finally flail out in delinquency and crime. What are we to expect from a hemisphere of youth where mounting frustrations are likely to fester into eruptions of violence and extremism? Annual per capita income in roughly half of the eighty underdeveloped nations that are members of the World Bank is rising by a paltry 1 percent a year or less. By the end of the century these nations, at their present rates of growth, will reach a per capita income of barely $170 a year. By the same criteria the United States will have attained a per capita income of $4,500.

The conclusion to all of this is inescapable. Given the certain connection between economic stagnation and the incidence of violence, the years that lie ahead for the nations in the southern half of the globe look ominous. This would be true even if no threat of Communist subversion existed, as it clearly does. Both Moscow and Peking, however harsh their internal differences, regard the modernization process as an ideal environment for the growth of Communism. Their experience with subversive internal war is extensive, and they have developed a considerable array of both doctrine and practical measures in the art of political violence.

It is clearly understood that certain Communist nations are capable of subverting, manipulating and finally directing for their own ends the wholly legitimate grievances of a developing society. But it would be a gross oversimplification to regard Communism as the central factor in every conflict throughout the underdeveloped world. Of the 149 serious internal insurgencies in those eight years under discussion, Communists were involved in only 58 of them, 38 percent of the total, and this includes 7 instances in which a Communist regime was itself the target of the uprising. Whether Communists are involved or not, violence anywhere in a taut world threatens the security and stability of nations half a globe away.

But neither conscience nor sanity itself suggests that the United States is, should or could be the Global Gendarme. Quite the contrary, experience confirms what human nature suggests, that in most instances of internal violence the local people themselves are best able to deal directly with the situation within the framework of their own traditions. The United States has no mandate from on high to police the world and no inclination to do so. There have been classic cases in which our own deliberate non-action was the wisest action of all. Where our help is not sought, it is seldom prudent to volunteer.

Certainly we have no charter to rescue floundering regimes which have brought violence on themselves by deliberately refusing to meet the legitimate expectations of their citizenry. Further, throughout the next decade advancing technology will reduce the requirement for bases and staging rights at particular locations abroad, and the whole pattern of forward deployment will gradually change. Though all these caveats are clear enough, the irreducible fact remains that our security is related directly to the security of the newly developing world, and our role must be precisely this, to help provide security to those developing nations which genuinely need and request our help and which demonstrably are willing and able to help themselves. The rub is that we do not always grasp the meaning of security in this context.

In a modernizing society security means development. Security is not military hardware, though it may include it; security is not military force, though it may involve it; security is not traditional military activity, though it may encompass it. Security is development, and without development there can be no security. A developing nation that does not, in fact, develop simply cannot remain secure for the intractable reason that its own citizenry cannot shed its human nature.

If security implies anything, it implies a minimal measure of order and stability. Without internal development of at least a minimal degree, order and stability are impossible. They are impossible because human nature cannot be frustrated indefinitely. It reacts because it must; that is what we do not always understand and what governments of modernizing nations do not always understand.

But by emphasizing that security arises from development I do not deny that an underdeveloped nation can be subverted from within or be the victim of aggression from without or be victim of a combination of the two. This can happen, and to prevent any or all of these conditions a nation does require appropriate military capabilities to deal with the specific problem.

The specific military problem, however, is only a narrow facet of the broader security problem. Military force can help provide law and order, but only to the degree that a basis for law and order already exists in the developing society, a basic willingness on the part of the people to cooperate. Law and order is the shield behind which development, the central fact of security, can be achieved.

We are not playing a semantic game with these words; the trouble is that we have been lost in a semantic jungle for too long and have come to identify security with exclusively military phenomena and most particularly with military hardware. It just isn't so, and we need to accommodate ourselves to the facts of the matter if we want to see security survive and grow in the southern half of the globe.

Development means economic, social and political progress. It means a reasonable standard of living, and reasonable in this context requires continual redefinition; what is reasonable in an earlier stage of development will become unreasonable in a later stage. As development progresses, security progresses, and when the people of a nation have organized their own human and natural resources to provide themselves with what they need and expect out of life, and have learned to compromise peacefully among competing demands in the larger national interest, then their resistance to disorder and violence will enormously increase. Conversely, the tragic need of desperate men to resort to force to achieve the inner imperatives of human decency will diminish.

I have mentioned that the role of the United States must be to help provide security to these modernizing nations, providing they need and request our help and are clearly willing and able to help themselves. But what should our help be? Clearly it should be help toward development. In the military sphere that involves two broad categories of assistance. We must help the developing nation with such training and equipment as are necessary to maintain the protective shield behind which development can go forward. The dimensions of that shield must vary from country to country. What is essential, though, is that it be a shield and not a capacity for external aggression.

The second and perhaps less understood category of military assistance in a modernizing nation is training in civic action, another one of those semantic puzzles. Too few Americans and too few officials in developing nations really comprehend what military civic action means. Essentially, it means using indigenous military forces for nontraditional military projects, projects that are useful to the local population in fields such as education, public works, health, sanitation and agriculture—indeed, anything connected with economic or social progress.

It has had some impressive results. In a recent four-year

period around the world U.S.-assisted civic-action programs constructed or repaired more than ten thousand miles of roads, built over a thousand schools and hundreds of hospitals and clinics, and provided medical and dental care to approximately four million people. What is important is that all this was done by indigenous men in uniform, and quite apart from the projects themselves the program powerfully alters the negative image of the military man as the oppressive preserver of the stagnant status quo.

Assistance in the purely military sense, though, is far from enough; economic assistance is essential. President Johnson has been determined that U.S. aid be hardheaded and realistic, that it must deal directly with the roots of underdevelopment and not merely attempt to alleviate the symptoms. The principle of the entire aid program is that U.S. economic help, no matter what its magnitude, is futile unless the country in question is resolute in making the primary effort itself. That is the criterion and ought to be the crucial condition for all our future assistance.

Only the developing nations themselves can take the fundamental measures that make outside assistance meaningful. These measures are often unpalatable and frequently call for political courage and decisiveness. But to fail to undertake painful but essential reform inevitably leads to far more painful revolutionary violence. Our economic assistance is designed to offer a reasonable alternative to that violence. It is designed to help substitute peaceful progress for tragic internal conflict.

The United States intends to be compassionate and generous in this effort, but it is not an effort it can carry exclusively by itself. Thus it must look to those nations which have reached the point of self-sustaining prosperity to increase their contribution to the development and thus to the security of the modernizing world.

This brings us to the second set of relationships that I mentioned at the outset: it is the policy of the United States to encourage and achieve a more effective partnership with those nations which can and should share international peace-keeping responsibilities. America has devoted a higher proportion of its Gross National Product to its military establishment than any other major free world nation and this was true even before our increased expenditures in Southeast Asia. Over the last few years we have had as many men in uniform as all the nations of Western Europe combined, though they have a population half again greater than our own.

The American people are not going to shirk their obligations in any part of the world, but clearly they cannot be expected to bear a disproportionate share of the common burden indefinitely. If, for example, other nations really believe, as they say they do, that it is in the common interest to deter the expansion of Red China's economic and political control beyond its national boundaries, then they must take a more active role in guarding the defense perimeter.

Let me be perfectly clear. This is not to question the policy of neutralism or nonalignment of any particular nation. Rather it is to emphasize that the independence of such nations can in the end be fully safeguarded only by collective agreements among themselves and their neighbors. The day is coming when no one nation, however powerful, can undertake by itself to keep the peace outside its own borders. Regional and international organizations for peace-keeping are as yet rudimentary, but they must grow in experience and be strengthened by deliberate and practical cooperative action. The Organization of the American States in the Dominican Republic, the more than thirty nations contributing troops or supplies to assist the Government of South Vietnam, indeed even the parallel efforts of the United States and the Soviet Union in the Pakistan-India conflict—these efforts together with those of the UN are the first attempts to substitute multinational for unilateral policing of violence. They point to the peace-keeping patterns of the future. We must not merely applaud the idea; we must dedicate talent, resources and hard practical thinking to its implementation.

In Western Europe, an area whose burgeoning economic vitality stands as a monument to the wisdom of the Marshall Plan, the problems of security are neither static nor wholly new. Fundamental changes are under way, though certain inescapable realities remain.

The conventional forces of NATO, for example, still require a nuclear backstop far beyond the capability of any Western European nation to supply, and the United States, as I pointed out earlier, is fully committed to provide that major nuclear deterrent. The European members of the Alliance, however, have a natural desire to participate more actively in nuclear planning. A central task of the Alliance, therefore, is to work out the relationships and institutions through which shared nuclear planning can be effective. A practical and promising start has been made in the Special Committee of NATO Defense Ministers. Common planning and consultation are essential aspects of any sensible substitute to the unworkable and dangerous alternative of independent national nuclear forces within the Alliance, and even beyond the Alliance we must find the means to prevent the proliferation of nuclear weapons. That is a clear imperative.

Of course, there are risks in nonproliferation arrangements, but they cannot be compared with the infinitely greater risks that would arise out of the increase in national nuclear stockpiles. In the calculus of risk, to proliferate independent national nuclear forces is not simply an arithmetical addition of danger. We would not merely be adding up risks; we would be insanely multiplying them.

If we seriously intend to pass on a world to our children that is not threatened by nuclear holocaust, we must come to grips with the problem of proliferation. A reasonable nonproliferation agreement is feasible, for there is no adversary with whom we do not share a common interest in avoiding mutual destruction triggered by an irresponsible "nth" power.

We come now to the third and last set of relationships the United States must deal with, those with nations who might be tempted to take up arms against us. These relationships call for realism, but realism is not a hardened, inflexible, unimaginative attitude. The realistic mind is restlessly creative, free of naïve delusions but full of practical alternatives.

There *are* practical alternatives to our current relationships with both the Soviet Union and Red China. A vast ideological chasm separates us from them and, to a degree, separates them from one another. There is nothing to be gained from our seeking an ideological rapprochement. But breaching the isolation of great nations like Red China, even when that isolation is largely of their own making, reduces the danger of potentially catastrophic misunderstandings and increases the incentive on both sides to resolve disputes by reason rather than by force.

There exist many ways in which we can build bridges toward nations who would cut themselves off from meaningful contact with us. We can do so with properly balanced trade relations, diplomatic contacts, and in some cases even by exchanges of military observers. We have to know, though, where it is we want to place this bridge, what sort of traffic we want to travel over it, and on what mutual foundations the structure can be designed. There are no one-cliff bridges; if you are going to span a chasm, you have to rest the structure on both cliffs.

Cliffs, generally speaking, are rather hazardous places. Some people are afraid even to look over the edge, but in a thermonuclear world we cannot afford political acrophobia. President Johnson put the matter squarely: by building bridges to those who make themselves our adversaries "we can help gradually to create a community of interest, a community of trust and a community of effort."

With respect to a community of effort, let me suggest a

concrete proposal for our own present young generation in the United States. It is a committed and dedicated generation; it has proven that by its enormously impressive performance in the Peace Corps overseas and by its willingness to volunteer for a final assault on such poverty and lack of opportunity as still remain in our own country.

As matters stand, our present Selective Service System normally draws on only a minority of eligible young men. That is an inequity, and it seems to me that we could move toward remedying that inequity by asking every young person in the United States to give two years of service to his country, whether in one of the military services, in the Peace Corps or in some other volunteer developmental work at home or abroad. We could encourage other countries to do the same, and we could work out exchange programs much as the Peace Corps is already planning to do.

While this is not an altogether new suggestion, it has been criticized as inappropriate while we are engaged in a shooting war. I believe precisely the opposite to be the case; it is more appropriate now than ever, for it would underscore what our whole purpose is in Vietnam and, indeed, anywhere in the world where coercion or injustice or lack of decent opportunity holds sway. It would make meaningful the central concept of security, a world of decency and development where every man can feel that his personal horizon is rimmed with hope.

Mutual interest, mutual trust and mutual effort—these are the goals. Can we achieve these goals with the Soviet Union and with Red China? Can they achieve them with one another? The answer to these questions lies in the answer to an even more fundamental question: Who is man? Is he a rational animal? If he is, then the goals can ultimately be achieved; if he is not, then there is little point in making the effort.

All the evidence of history suggests that man is indeed a rational animal, but with a nearly infinite capacity for folly. His history seems largely a halting but persistent effort to raise his reason above his animality. He draws blueprints for Utopia but never quite gets it built. In the end he plugs away obstinately with the only building material really ever at hand: his own part-comic, part-tragic, part-cussed, part-glorious nature. I, for one, would not count a global free society out. Coercion, after all, merely captures man. Freedom captivates him.

Epilogue

AFTER more than a million years of life on earth man has at last reached a point where if he is to survive he must begin better to understand the intrinsic imperatives of security. There are two reasons why I believe he will.

First, the technological revolution has hurried history forward so rapidly in our own lifetime that we can now grasp more realistically the utter futility of unlimited war. A victory of sorts was possible in the first two unlimited world wars. No meaningful victory is even conceivable in a third unlimited world war, for no nation can possibly win a full-scale thermonuclear exchange. The two world powers that have now achieved a mutual assured-destruction capability fully realize that. And however imperfect may be the state of peace today, it is crucially important that there should be that full realization, for it results in restraint in lesser conflicts. The United States and the Soviet Union, though in serious confrontation with one another's objectives in the crisis situations in Berlin, Cuba, the Middle East and Vietnam, have acted—and continue to act—with a realistic degree of restraint. That is a significant step forward on the path to greater global rationality.

A significant step backward on that same path would be the further proliferation of nuclear weapons. For that process geometrically increases the risk of suicidal miscalculation. Sane leaders in sane nations have the strongest possible motive for prescribing every possible diplomatic antidote for the poison of proliferation. Reasonable agreements in this field *are* feasible, and must be pursued with relentless perseverance. The most profound problem the non-nuclear nations face is the psychological difficulty of comprehending the inherent futility of a nuclear arsenal in the face of the strategic realities and the requirement for political courage to act accordingly.

The second reason for my belief that security is more within man's grasp in our particular era—as permanently dangerous an era as it self-evidently remains—is that we are beginning better to understand that stability of relationships among rich nations is affected by the stability of the institutions of the poor nations. And, in the long run, stability in the poor nations is a function of development. That is obvious enough in the case of those impoverished nations whose peoples are seething with growing frustrations, nations racked with famine and disease and the cruel pressures of expanding populations on diminishing resources. But while we have begun to recognize the obvious correlation between social, economic and political stagnation and volcanic internal violence, we have yet to do enough about it. But I believe that we will begin to do more, and soon. We will do more because we will have to do more.

How many twilight wars of insurgency—wars feeding on the frustrations born of underdevelopment—the affluent nations will be content to witness before they take the only sensible steps possible to cure the malady at its source is problematical. Man does have the unhappy ability to stare at the obvious, and then deliberately to retreat into escapist delusions. He often does this in the case of unpleasant truths, only because that is more comforting in the short run than facing up to the arduous tasks at hand. But short-run delusions have a habit of turning into long-run regrets. The regrets stemming from the rich nations' delusions over the poor nations' problems are lengthening into the long-run stage now, and I am increasingly hopeful that at some point soon—and I say soon only because delay becomes more disastrous year after violent year—there will be a significant change of attitude. The wealthy and secure nations of the world will realize that they cannot possibly remain either wealthy or secure if they continue to close their eyes to the pestilence of poverty that covers the whole southern half of the globe. They will open their eyes and act, if only to preserve their own immunity from the infection.

The affluent nations that spend billions of dollars each year on military hardware will begin to question the growing disproportion between those immense sums and the relatively minuscule amounts devoted to developmental aid —not because the rich nations will suddenly become more philanthropic, but because they will gradually become more realistic. They will reach a point of realism at which it becomes clear that a dollar's worth more of military hardware will buy less security for themselves than a dollar's worth more of developmental assistance.

If they ponder the matter deeply, I believe the affluent nations of the Northern Hemisphere will conclude that they are close to that point of realism today. Just as collective security is the only sensible military strategy in a half-free and half-totalitarian world, so collective developmental assistance is the only sensible economic strategy in a half-fed and half-famished world. Collective security and collective development are but two faces of the same coin.

APPENDIX I

The Emerging Nuclear Capability of Red China

Chapter Four records my reasons for opposing the deployment of a $40 billion antiballistic-missile system. It is important, however, to distinguish between such an ABM system, designed to protect against a Soviet attack on our cities, and systems which have other objectives. One of the other uses of an ABM system which have seriously been considered is the greater protection of our strategic offensive forces. Another relates to the emerging nuclear capability of Communist China. There is evidence that the Chinese are devoting very substantial resources to the development of both nuclear warheads and missile-delivery systems. Indications are that they will have medium-range ballistic missiles soon, an initial intercontinental ballistic missile capability in the early 1970s, and a modest force in the mid-seventies.

Until recently, the lead-time factor allowed us to postpone a decision on whether or not a light ABM deployment might be needed as a countermeasure to Red China's nuclear development. China still is caught up in internal strife, but it seems likely that her basic motivation in developing a strategic nuclear capability is to provide a basis for threatening her neighbors, and to clothe herself with the dubious prestige that the world pays to nuclear weaponry. We deplore her development of these weapons, just as we deplore it in other countries. We oppose nuclear proliferation because we believe that in the end it only increases the risk of a common and cataclysmic holocaust.

President Johnson has made it clear that the United States will oppose any efforts of China to employ nuclear blackmail against her neighbors. We possess now, and will continue to possess for as far ahead as we can foresee, an overwhelming first-strike capability with respect to China. And despite the raucous propaganda to the effect that "the atomic bomb is a paper tiger," there is ample evidence that China well appreciates the destructive power of nuclear weapons. She has been cautious to avoid any action that might end in a nuclear clash with the United States, however wild her words, and understandably so. We have the power not only to destroy completely her entire nuclear offensive forces but to devastate her society as well.

Is there any possibility, then, that by the mid-1970s China might become so incautious as to attempt a nuclear attack on the United States or our allies? It would be suicidal for her to do so, but one can conceive conditions under which China might miscalculate. We wish to reduce such possibilities to a minimum. And since, as I have noted, our strategic planning must always be conservative, and take into consideration even the possible irrational behavior of potential adversaries, there are *marginal* grounds for concluding that a light deployment of U.S. ABMs against this possibility is prudent.

The system will be relatively inexpensive—preliminary estimates place the cost at about $5 billion—and will have a much higher degree of reliability against a Chinese attack than the much more massive and complicated system that some have recommended against a possible Soviet attack. Moreover, the light deployment will have a number of other advantages. It will provide an additional indication to Asians that we intend to deter China from nuclear blackmail, and thus contribute toward our goal of discouraging nuclear-weapon proliferation among the present nonnuclear countries. It will enable us to add as a concurrent benefit a further defense of our Minuteman sites against Soviet attack, which means that at modest cost we would, in fact, be adding even greater effectiveness to our offensive missile force and avoiding a much more costly expansion of that force. Finally, such a reasonably reliable ABM system will add protection of our population against the improbable but possible accidental launching of an intercontinental missile by any one of the nuclear powers.

After a detailed review of all these considerations, we decided in late 1967 to go forward with this Chinese-oriented ABM deployment, and actual production of the system began before the end of the year. In reaching this decision, we realized that it contained two possible dangers, and we must guard carefully against both. The first is that we may lapse psychologically into the old oversimplification about the adequacy of nuclear power. The simple truth is that nuclear weapons can serve to deter only a narrow range of threats. This ABM deployment will strengthen our defensive posture and will enhance the effectiveness of our land-based ICBM forces. But the independent nations of Asia must realize that these benefits are no substitute for their maintaining, and where necessary strengthening, their own conventional forces in order to deal with the more likely threats to the security of the region.

The second danger is also psychological. There is a kind of mad momentum intrinsic to the development of all new nuclear weaponry. If a weapons system works and works well, there is strong pressure from many directions to procure and deploy the weapon out of all proportion to the prudent level required. The danger in deploying this relatively light and reliable Chinese-oriented ABM system is going to be that pressures will develop to expand it into a heavy Soviet-oriented ABM system. We must resist that temptation firmly. We cannot for a moment afford to relax our vigilance against a possible Soviet first strike. But our greatest deterrent against such a strike is not a massive, costly and highly penetrable ABM shield, but rather a fully credible, offensive, assured-destruction capability.

Our decision to go ahead with a limited ABM deployment in no way indicates that we feel agreement with the Soviet Union on the limitation of strategic nuclear forces is any less urgent or desirable.

APPENDIX II

Sources

As the Preface made clear, this volume was drawn from a variety of sources, including both my public addresses and declassified portions of reports to Congress. Basic sources for each chapter were as follows:

Chapters One, Two and Three: statement by the Secretary of Defense to the Congress on the 1969–73 Defense Program and the 1969 Defense Budget, January, 1968; summary of remarks prepared for the North Atlantic Council of Foreign and Defense Ministers, December, 1967.

Chapter Four: address, United Press International Editors and Publishers, San Francisco, September 18, 1967.

Chapter Five: statements to the Congress.

Chapter Six: address, American Society of Newspaper Editors, Washington, April 20, 1963.

Chapter Seven: address, Chatham College, Pittsburgh, May 22, 1966; address, Millsaps College, Jackson, Mississippi, February 24, 1967.

Chapter Eight: address, Veterans of Foreign Wars, New

York, August 23, 1966; address, Plans for Progress Conference, Washington, October 3, 1967; address, National Association of Educational Broadcasters, Denver, November 7, 1967.

Chapter Nine: address, American Society of Newspaper Editors, Montreal, May 18, 1966.

INDEX

ABM, *see* Antiballistic missile system
Africa
  poverty of, 130
  security interests of NATO in, 28
Algeria, 26, 27
Alliance for Progress, 30
Alliances, success of interlocking, 5
Americans, disillusionment of, 11
Antiballistic missile system (ABM), 62-66, 163-66
  arms race and, 65
  assured-destruction capability and, 62, 63
  China and deployment of, 163-66
  Soviet Union and deployment of, 62-66, 165, 166
  warhead penetration of, 78
ANZUS, 5
Aquinas, St. Thomas, 134
Aristotle, 117, 134
Arms race, 58-62
  ABM and, 65
  basis for, 58-59
  continuation of, 60-61
  folly of, 67
  as means to end, 62
Asia, poverty in, 130
Asia and Pacific Council, 22
Asian Development Bank, 22
Association of Southeast Asian Nations, 23

Assured-destruction capability, 160
  ABM and, 62, 63
  credibility of, 52-53
  definition of, 52
  gross megatonnage and, 56
  need to maintain, 76
  size of forces for, 77
Atlas (missiles), 72-73
Augustine, St., 116

Berlin (West)
  crisis in, 12, 160
  nuclear power and, 59
Bolivia, 29
Brain drain, 108-9
B-70 (aircraft), controversy over, 91-92

California, open housing in, 126
Canada, peace between U.S. and, 142-43
Castro, Fidel, revolution and, 14-15
China (Red)
  Cultural Revolution in, 17-19
  direction and potential of, 12-13
  economic stagnation and, 147-48
  expansion of, 153
  future regimes in, 19-20
  India and
    border dispute, 16
    objectives in India of, 25-26
  interests in Southeast Asia of, 20-22
  nuclear system of, 75-77

China (Red) (*continued*)
  setbacks to, 14
  Soviet Union and Sino-Soviet dispute, 14-16
    Soviet Union as moderating influence on, 20
  tolerance-to-damage of, 76
  U. S. and
    ABM deployment by U. S., 163-66
    changes in relations, 156, 157
    containment of, 5
    diplomatic relations, 20
    war between, 164-65
  Western statesmanship and, 13
  world revolution and, 14-15
  See also Communism
China, Republic of (Taiwan), 5, 25
Cold War, ideologies of, 10
Collective defense, 3-11
  Congress and, 8-10
  isolationism and, 6-7
  1967 setback in, 8-10
  principle of, 4
  ultimate goal of, 5-6
  See also ANZUS; NATO; Rio Treaty; SEATO
Colonialism, as technological gap, 108
Common Market, 35
  technological gap and, 108
Communism
  division in world of, 13-14
  economic stagnation and, 147-48
  multiple centers of, 3-4
  promise vs. reality of, 5
Congress, collective defense and, 8-10
Conflicts
  national wealth and, 146
  quantity of *de facto*, 145
Conventional forces, 81-85
  growth of, 81-82
  logistic system for, 84-85
  mobility of, 82-84
  re-evaluation of (1961), 78-79
  Strategic Reserve and, 80
  use of, 79

Cuba, 12, 160
  insurgency sponsored by, 29
Cultural Revolution, Great, 17-19

Defense, Department of, 88-104
  bilineal organizational structure of, 96-97
  budget, 93-94
    budgetary grouping of defense needs by, 90-91
    cost of developing weapons and, 91-94
    cost reduction program, 89
    Planning-Programing-Budgeting-System of, 94-95
    savings, 101-3
    systems-analysis staff of, 95-96
  challenge to, 87
  creation of (1947), 96
  efficiency in, 88-89
    motivation for efficiency, 100-1
  gravest problem of, 51
  managing of, x-xi
    axioms to managing, 88
  military and
    logistics management, 98-100
    military effectiveness and, 89-90
    organization of Joint Chiefs of Staff by, 97-98
  mission of, 122
  national interest and, 103-4
    core conclusions on national defense and, x-xi
    principles in directing national defense, viii-ix
  number of people employed by, vii
  social programs of, *see* Social programs
Democracy, management and, 109, 119
Deterrence, 51-67
  ABM as
    arms race and, 65
    assured-destruction capability of, 62, 63

Deterrence (*continued*)
  China and deployment of, 163-66
  Soviet Union and deployment of, 62-66, 165, 166
  arms race and, 58-62
    ABM and, 65
    basis for arms race, 58-59
    continuation of, 60-61
    folly of, 67
    as means to end, 62
  assured-destruction capability in, 160
    ABM and, 62, 63
    credibility of, 52-53
    definition of, 52
    gross megatonnage and, 56
    need to maintain, 76
    size of forces for, 77
  cornerstone of, 75-76
  decline of non-nuclear force for, 70-71
  enlarging arsenal for, 57-58
  first-strike capability in, 53-55
    against Soviet Union, 55
    arms race and, 60-61
    arsenal and, 62
    definition of, 52-54
  graduated, 60
  ICBM in, 57-58
  limited role of nuclear, 59-60
  manned bombers for, 71-74
  second-strike capability in
    arms race and, 60-61
    arsenal and, 62
    definition of, 55
    of U.S. and Soviet Union, 55-56
  warheads and, 56-57
  See also Collective defense; Conventional forces; Weapons systems
Developing nations, 144-52
  Communism and, 147-48
  economic gap and, 146-47
  floundering regimes in, 148-49
  increasing numbers of conflicts in, 145
  number of, 144
  problems of, 144-45
  stability for, 160-61
  U.S. aid to, 151-52
  wealth of, 146
Dominican Republic, 154
Draft, Project 100,000 and, 127-28, 131-38

Economic gap, widening of, 146-147
Education
  draft and deficiency in, 128; *see also* Draft
  need for, 112-13
  relevancy of, 117-18
  Project 100,000 and, 131-34
  U.S. compared with European, 111-12
  of youth, 120-21
Equal opportunity, Defense Department and, 124-25
Eisenhower, Dwight D., 65
Europe
  decline of threat to, 32-33
  educational weakness of, 111-12
  industrial gap between U.S. and, 110
  non-nuclear defense of, 45-47
  peace-keeping and, 153, 154
  Soviet Union and, 35-36
  technological gap and, 108-9

First-strike capability
  against Soviet Union, 55
  arms race and, 60-61
  arsenal and, 62
  definition of, 53-54
Five-Year Cost Reduction Program (1962), 89
Five-Year Defense Program, 95
France
  education in, 111-12
  position on NATO of, 36
Frost, Robert, 120

Gaps, *see* Economic gap; Technological gap
Geneva Accords on Laos (1962), 24

Germany (West)
  education in, 111
  industrialization of, 111
  NATO and, 33, 36, 40, 42
Gesell, Gerhard A., 123, 124
Great Britain, *see* United Kingdom
Great Leap Forward, 18
Greece
  NATO and, 33
  U.S. aid to, 27-28
Gross National Product, military
  expenditures and, 153
Guevara, Ernesto Che, 29

Housing, open, for armed forces,
  123-27

ICBM, *see* Intercontinental bal-
  listic missiles
India, 15
  China and
    border dispute, 16
    objectives in India of, 25-26
    conflict with Pakistan of, 25-26,
      154
  Soviet Union and
    aid to India, 26
    India-Pakistan conflict, 154
  U.S. military aid to, 25
Indonesia, 14, 25
Intercontinental ballistic missiles
  (ICBM)
  ABM and, 166
  attack by, 71-72
  in deterrence, 57-58
  quantity of, 73-75
Iraq, 26
Iran, 27
Isolationism, possibility of return
  to, 6-7
Israel, 16
Italy, education in, 111

Japan, 5
  industrialization of, 111
  military defense of, 30, 31
Jefferson, Thomas, 117
Johnson, Lyndon B., 65, 88, 143,
  152

China and, 164
  on community of interests be-
    tween nations, 156
Joint Chiefs of Staff, 95-98

Kennedy, John F., 65, 88, 143
Khrushchev, Nikita, 33
Korea (North), 21, 24-25
  war in, 6, 59
Korea (South), 24-25
  defense agreements with, 5
  war in, 6, 59

Laos, 15
  conflict in, 23-24
Latin America, 14, 31
  armed insurgency in, 29-30
  military policy toward, 28-29
  poverty in, 130
  world revolution and, 14-15
Logistics
  conventional forces and, 84-85
  management of, 98-100

Management, 109-12
  democracy and, 109, 119
  education for, 111-12
  importance of, 109-10
Mao Tse-tung, 18-19
Marshall Plan, 154
Maryland, open housing for armed
  forces in, 126
Mekong Development Project, 22
Middle East, 15, 25, 160
  Soviet penetration into, 26-28
  turmoil in (1967), 26-27
Minuteman (missile launchers)
  ABM and, 63
  build-up of (1961), 58
  deployment of, 72-73, 75, 165
  quantity of, 54
Missile systems, *see* ABM; Atlas;
    ICBM; Minuteman; Nike-
    Zeus; Polaris; Poseidon; Reg-
    ulus; Titan
Morocco, 28

Nationalism, 108-9
National liberation, wars of, 14

National Military Command System, 75
National Security Act (1947), 88, 96
NATO, *see* North Atlantic Treaty Organization
Nike-Zeus (missiles), 74
North Atlantic Treaty Organization (NATO), 5, 32-47, 108
  background to, 33
  changes in, 37
  forces of, 79-81
    military needs of, 39-40
    nuclear planning in, 154-55
    nuclear weaponry in, 86
    nuclear backstop to, 154
    reserves for, 42-44
  France's position on, 36
  Germany and, 33, 36, 40, 42
  limited aggression and, 37-38
  need to maintain, 35-36
  new flexibility of, 45-47
  rifts in Communist world and defense of, 14
  security interests in Africa of, 28
  Soviet Union and, 33-42
    creation of NATO and, 33
    NATO as deterrence to, 35-37
    U.S. commitment to NATO and, 37-39
  success of, 32
  utility of, 34
Nuclear war
  with China, 164-65
  as deterrence on Soviet policy, 4
  futility of, 159
  limitations as instrument of policy of, 12
  planning for, 51
  specificity of, 69
  strategy for, *see* Deterrence
  undesirability of, 52

Open housing in armed forces, 123-127
Organization of American States, 154

Pakistan, 15
  conflict with India of, 25-26, 154
  U.S. military aid to, 25
Peace Corps, 157
Philippines, 5
Phouma, Souvanna, 24
Planning-Programing-Budgeting-System, 94-95
Polaris (missiles), 72-73, 75, 86
  build-up of (1961), 58
  quantity of, 54
Policeman, U.S. as world, 7-8, 148
Population explosion, 119
Poseidon (missiles), 86
  ABM and, 63
Poverty
  characteristics of, 128-29
  national security and, 122-23
  Project 100,000 and, 127-28, 131-138
  social unrest caused by, 129-30
  as waste of talent, 130-31
  will to achievement and, 135
  world, 161; *see also* Developing nations
Protest, Age of, 113
Public, participation in security matters of, vii-viii

Racial discrimination, 123-25
Red Guards, 18, 19
Regulus (missiles), 73
Revolution, *see* World revolution
Rio Treaty (1947), 5
  armed insurgency and, 29
Roosevelt, Franklin D., 47
Russia, *see* Soviet Union

SEATO (Southeast Asia Treaty Organization), 5
Second-strike capability
  arms race and, 60-61
  arsenal and, 62
  definition of, 55
  of U.S. and Soviet Union, 55-56
Security
  as economic development, 149-150

Security (*continued*)
  narrow notion of, 141-42
  poverty and, 122-23
  public participation in, vii-viii
Selective Service System, 157; *see also* Draft
Social injustice, national security and, 122-23
Social organization, growing complexity of, 120
Social programs, 123-40
  open housing as, 123-27
  Project 100,000 as, 127-28, 131-138
  Project Transition as, 138-40
South America, *see* Latin America
Southeast Asia, *see* Laos; Thailand; Vietnam
Southeast Asia Treaty Organization (SEATO), 5
Soviet Union
  accommodation with, 4
  China and
    Sino-Soviet dispute, 14-16
    Soviet Union as moderating influence on, 20
  constructive behavior of, 15-16
  containment of, 5
  defense expenditures of, 17
  deterrence capability of, 160
    ABM deployment and, 62-66, 165, 166
    first-strike capability of, 54-55, 60-61
    nuclear arsenal of, 54, 56-59
    second-strike capability of, 55-56
    warheads and, 57
  economic stagnation and, 147-48
  Europe and, 35-36
  India and
    aid to India, 26
    India-Pakistan conflict and, 154
  interests in Southeast Asia of, 20-22
  Middle East and
    penetration into Middle East, 26-28

    turmoil (1967) in, 26-27
  NATO and, 33-42
    creation of NATO and, 33
    NATO as deterrence to, 35-37
    U.S. commitment to, 37-39
  political and military developments of, 16-17
  restraint of, in support of North Vietnam, 14, 15
  setbacks to, 14
  U.S. and
    changes in relations, 156, 157
    conflicting interests, 12, 15
  Western statesmanship and, 13
  world revolution and, 14-15
  See also Communism
Students
  protests of, 113-15
  refreshing quality of ferment among, 117
  Vietnam war and demonstrations by, 113
Syria, 26, 27

Technological gap, 107-13
  brain drain and, 108
  as colonialism, 108
  education as closing of, 110-13
  Europe and, 108-9
  as managerial gap, 109-10
Technology, 117
  fear of, 114-16
Thailand, 23
Titan (missiles), 72-73
Trewhitt, Henry, viii
Truman, Harry S., 123
Tunisia, 28
Turkey, 27
  NATO and, 33

United Arab Republic (U.A.R.), 26, 27
United Kingdom, 35, 108
  education in, 111
  NATO and, 36
United Nations, 26, 154
  charter of, 5

United States
ABM and, 62-66, 163-66
arms race and, 65
assured-destruction capability
and, 62, 63
China and deployment of, 163-
166
Soviet Union and deployment
of, 62-66, 165, 166
warhead penetration of, 78
aid to developing nations, 151-52
aid to Greece, 27-28
arms race and, 58-62
ABM and, 65
basis for, 58-59
continuation of, 60-61
folly of, 67
as means to end, 62
assured-destruction capability of,
160
ABM and, 62, 63
credibility of, 52-53
definition of, 52
gross megatonnage and, 56
need to maintain, 76
size of forces for, 77
China and
ABM deployment by U.S., 163-
166
changes in relations, 156, 157
containment of, 5
diplomatic relations, 20
war between, 164-65
deterrence capability of, 51-67
combat readiness of, 144
cornerstone of, 75-76
decline of non-nuclear force
for, 70-71
enlarging arsenal for, 57-58
graduated, 60
ICBM in, 57-58
limited role of nuclear, 59-60
manned bombers for, 71-74
nuclear strength of, 54, 141
warhead and, 56-57
See also Collective defense;
Conventional forces; Weapons system

United States (*continued*)
draft in, 128; *see also* Draft
European education compared
with, 111-12
financial support to allies of, 8
first-strike capability of,
against Soviet Union, 55
arms race and, 60-61
arsenal and, 62
definition of, 53-54
ICBMs and
ABM and, 166
attack by, 71-72
in deterrence, 57-58
quantity of, 73-75
industrial gap between Europe
and, 110
isolationism in, 6-7
Middle East and, 26, 27
military aid to India and Pakistan
by, 25
NATO and, 33-35
commitment to NATO, 37-39
new flexibility of NATO and,
45-47
nations opposed to, 155-57
as Pacific power, 22
peace between Canada and, 142-
143
peace-keeping responsibilities of,
153-54
policy in Southeast Asia, 22-23
poverty in, 129, 130
pre-eminence of, 11
proposal to youth of, 157
second-strike capability of
arms race and, 60-61
arsenal and, 62
definition of, 55
of U.S. and Soviet Union, 55-
56
Soviet Union and
changes in relations, 156, 157
conflicting interests, 12, 15
technological gap and, 109
unique interests of, 12
wealth of, 146
as world policeman, 7-8, 148

U.S.S.R., *see* Soviet Union

Vietnam (North)
  conflict with, 4
  conflict of China and Soviet
    Union over, 20-22
  infiltration into Laos of, 23-24
  Soviet restraint in support of, 14,
    15
  war aid to, 13
Vietnam (South), war in, 15, 22,
  160
  forces sent to (1965), 80
  nations involved in, 154
  Negro casualty rate in (1967),
    125
  student demonstrations and, 113
Virginia, open housing for armed
  forces in, 126

War, *see* Nuclear war
Washington (D.C.), open housing
  for armed forces in, 126
Weapons systems, 68-86
  B-70 in, 91-92
  development costs of, 91-92
  limitations of nuclear, 69-70
  Nike-Zeus, 74
  non-nuclear, 78-86
  restraint in choosing new, 92-93
  tactical nuclear, 69
  use of nuclear, 70-78
  See also ABM; ICBM
West Germany, *see* Germany
Wilson, Harold, 108
World Bank, 146, 147
World revolution, 14-15

Yemen, 27